Ford Taurus
in NASCAR

How Ford's Best-Selling Sedan Became
NASCAR's Hottest Racing Machine

By Bill Center
Foreword by Ned Jarrett

HarperEntertainment

A Division of HarperCollinsPublishers

www.harpercollins.com

A TEHABI BOOK

////// **NASCAR**

www.nascar.com

Ford Taurus
in NASCAR

How Ford's Best-Selling Sedan Became
NASCAR's Hottest Racing Machine

By Bill Center
Foreword by Ned Jarrett

TEHABI BOOKS

Ford Taurus in NASCAR was produced by Tehabi Books. *Tehabi*—symbolizing the spirit of teamwork—derives its name from the Hopi Indian tribe of the southwestern United States. As an award-winning book producer, Tehabi works with national and international publishers, corporations, institutions, and nonprofit groups to identify, develop, and implement comprehensive publishing programs. Tehabi Books is located in Del Mar, California.

www.tehabi.com

Chris Capen, *President*
Tom Lewis, *Editorial and Design Director*
Sharon Lewis, *Controller*
Nancy Cash, *Managing Editor*
Andy Lewis, *Senior Art Director*
Sarah Morgans, *Associate Editor*
Mo Latimer, *Editorial Assistant*
Maria Medina, *Administrative Assistant*
Kevin Giontzeneli, *Production Artist*
Curtis Boyer, *Production Artist*
Sam Lewis, *Webmaster*
Ross Eberman, *Director of Custom Publishing*
Tim Connolly, *Sales and Marketing Manager*
Eric Smith, *Marketing Assistant*
Tiffany Smith, *Executive Assistant*
Gail Fink, *Copy Editor*
Linda Bannan, *Proofreader*

CAPITONS
Pages 2-3:
Jeremy Mayfield powers his Ford Taurus up the hill just after the starting line on the road course at Sears Point Raceway in Sonoma, California.

Page 5:
Elliott Sadler (21) challenges Rusty Wallace in a Taurus-to-Taurus duel coming off a turn at Rockingham, North Carolina.

Pages 6-7:
The background is a blur as the camera freeze-frames the Ford Taurus driven by Mark Martin.

HarperEntertainment
A Division of HarperCollinsPublishers

Ford Taurus in NASCAR was published by HarperEntertainment, a Division of HarperCollins Publishers Inc., 10 East 53rd Street, New York, NY 10022.

John Silbersack, *Senior Vice President and Publishing Director*
Mark Landau, *Vice President, Special Sales, Key Account Development*
Frank Fochetta, *Vice President and Director of HarperCollins Enterprises*
Amy Wasserman, *Marketing Director*
Susan Sanguily, *Creative Director*

www.harpercollins.com

HarperCollins books may be purchased for educational, business, or sales promotional use. For information please write: Special Markets Department, HarperCollins Publishers Inc., 10 East 53rd Street, New York, NY 10022.

Photography credits appear on page 132.

Library of Congress Cataloging-in-Publication Data is available from the Librarian, HarperCollins Publishers, Inc., 10 East 53rd Street, New York, NY 10022.
ISBN 0-06-105175-6 (trade ed.)
ISBN 0-06-105176-4 (corporate ed.)

This edition is printed on acid-free paper that meets the American National Standards Institute Z39.48 Standard.
Printed in the United States through R.R. Donnelley & Sons Company.

Contents

The sport of auto racing is about many things.

It's about teamwork and talent, ingenuity and hard work, late nights and never giving up. But, at the end of the day, it's mostly about winning the battle.

Sometimes that battle is a two-lap shootout. Or a 500-mile race for the championship. And sometimes that battle is an eight-month struggle to do what your competition thinks is impossible.

The development of the Ford Taurus race car was that sort of battle. It's the story of a lot of people who refused to listen to what the skeptics had to say. It's a story about people who believed in themselves, in each other, and in the mission to get a new race car ready to debut at Daytona in February 1998.

Consider this: Chevrolet took more than two years to develop the Monte Carlo race car before it debuted in 1995. Ford asked its teams to work with its engineers to develop the Ford Taurus in less than one year. And for good measure, it had to be a winning car right away, because in the competitive world of NASCAR Winston Cup racing, anything less is unacceptable.

So this is the story of a group of Ford engineers, Ford race teams, and Ford drivers. People who compete with each other every week on the race track—all coming together with one purpose, to do what they do best—winning the battle.

Like any challenge, there were squabbles, disagreements, and differences of opinion, but in the end, everyone remained focused on the same goals: Taurus. Daytona. Winning.

As you read through this book, you will be tempted to think that this is only the story of a race car. The NASCAR Taurus. Winner of fifteen races in its debut season. The model of choice for twenty of the world's finest racers.

Don't be fooled.

The NASCAR Taurus story is about people . . . the people who drove Taurus to its debut in Daytona, and the people who keep driving it to Victory Lane.

It was a worthy battle, a great race . . . and a wonderful story.

I know you'll enjoy it.

The Jarretts of North Carolina, opposite, are Ford's first family on the NASCAR Winston Cup Series. Father Ned (left) was the first driver to win the season driver's championship for Ford in 1965 and he won a total of forty-three races in Fords. A second victory in the Brickyard 400 on August, 7, 1999, in a Taurus extended son Dale's (right) lead in the NASCAR Winston Cup standings.

The Battle
by Ned Jarrett

or Henry Ford, the dream of producing cars for the public began with a race. Five years after he built his first automobile, Ford still hadn't found a way to attract attention to his product. He saw his chance in a ten-mile race scheduled for October 10, 1901, at Grosse Pointe, Michigan. The winner was to get $1,000 and, Ford astutely believed, public exposure. He desperately needed both.

Ford had never raced a car before. His opponent, Alexander Winton, was considered the best racer of the time. And Winton, as expected, quickly pulled away to a 200-yard lead on the one-mile dirt oval owned by the Detroit Driving Club. But Ford's machine was faster on the straights. And by mid-race, with mechanic Spider Huff leaning out of the car on the turns to give it more balance, Ford started closing on Winton. Ford took the lead with two laps to go and won with the average speed of 44.8 mph.

Ford never raced again. But Fords did.

Cars carrying the banner of the Ford Motor Company have competed in almost every venue known to racing throughout the twentieth century. Fords have won at Indianapolis and Le Mans, Monaco and Baja. And for the past fifty years, Fords have been part of NASCAR. Fords were there from the start: Jim Roper drove a Lincoln to victory in NASCAR's first Strictly Stock race at the Charlotte, North Carolina, fairgrounds on June 19, 1949.

But it wasn't always like it is today.

During NASCAR's formative years, the Ford factory took a hands-off approach watching from the sidelines as a small group of loyalists raced Fords. That began to change in 1955 when Ford executives noticed that a Sunday success on the track computed into Monday sales in the showroom. In 1955, Robert McNamara, general manager of the Ford Division, decided Ford should—as a company—go stock car racing. That decision

Henry Ford

The History of Ford Racing in NASCAR

set in motion one of the greatest sagas in motorsports history. It is a story rich in names as well as victories. The Ford drivers and owners read like a Who's Who of racing: Peter DePaolo, John Holman, Ralph Moody, the Wood Brothers, Curtis Turner, David Pearson, Bud Moore, Ned Jarrett, Bill Elliott, Junior Johnson, Cale Yarburough, Alan Kulwicki, Davey Allison, Fred Lorenzen, Mark Martin, Jack Roush, Robert Yates, Jeff Burton, Dale Jarrett, and thousands more.

And the triumphs—On October 25, 1998, Rusty Wallace recorded a milestone 15th victory for the new Ford Taurus in the model's first year in the NASCAR Winston Cup Series. When Dale Jarrett won at Indianapolis on August 7, 1999, it was the 495th triumph for Ford at NASCAR's highest level—dating back to Jim Roper's implausible victory in 1949. Implausible because Roper was more of a dreamer than a die-hard racer. He had read about NASCAR's first race in a newspaper comic strip and had driven his sturdy Lincoln to Charlotte from Great Bend, Kansas, to be part of the show. Roper's triumph set the stage for future Ford dreamers. And they dreamed big.

Programs set forth by Peter DePaolo and the team of John Holman and Ralph Moody in the mid-1950s became standards of excellence that stand today. And it all started with a phone call by McNamara, who would later become the secretary of defense. Impressed by media coverage that Chevrolet and Chrysler had gained through their racing programs and concerned that Ford might lose its edge in the youth market it had dominated for decades, McNamara hastily commissioned a two-car

A Ford Fairlane driven by Bobby Lee slides through a turn in the last race run on the famed Beach-Road course at Daytona Beach, Florida, in 1958.

Ford effort for the 1955 Southern 500 at Darlington, South Carolina. During the race, the Fords, driven by Curtis Turner and Joe Weatherly, both led before retiring with suspension failures.

Ford became hooked on stock car racing. But the factory decided it needed a professional to run its racing operations. Enter DePaolo, winner of the 1925 Indianapolis 500 and one of the brightest minds in racing. Ford designated DePaolo Engineering to be its racing arm. Peter DePaolo was in charge of signing everyone from mechanics to drivers. He had a keen eye for talent. Soon the

The Ford Fairlane of Mario Andretti (11) passed David Pearson (6) en route to winning the 1967 Daytona 500. Five seasons later, Darrell Waltrip made his NASCAR Winston Cup debut in Andretti's Daytona 500 winner.

Following spread, two of Ford's leading all-time drivers battled on the banks of Daytona International Speedway. Fred Lorenzen (28) and Junior Johnson (27) tied for fifth on the all-time list of Ford winners with twenty-six victories. Lorenzen drove a Ford to victory in the 1965 Daytona 500.

likes of Ralph Moody, John Holman, and Bill Stroppe were working for Ford, and the drivers included Fireball Roberts, Marvin Panch, Weatherly, and Turner. By the time Ford returned to the Southern 500 in 1956, it was no longer an upstart operation; it was a formidable team. Turner won the seventh Southern 500 by a margin of two laps. Marvin Panch was third. And Ford was rolling.

Prior to 1956, Ford—including the Mercury and Lincoln Divisions—had won a total of eleven races in NASCAR's first seven years of Strictly Stock and Grand National racing, although a number of drivers ran Fords in NASCAR's Modified Division. However, 1956 was a breakout season; Fords and Mercurys won nineteen Grand National races and Ford won twenty-seven of the forty-eight events in NASCAR's new Convertible Division. Ford's domination continued early in 1957. Fords won fifteen of NASCAR's first twenty-one Grand National races and seventeen of the first twenty convertible races. Then, on June 6, 1957, the Automobile Manufacturers Association—a group that included Ford, General Motors, and Chrysler—voted to ban factory-sponsored racing teams out of fears that the public's growing love of racing and horsepower adversely affected the industry's public image.

Less than two years after getting into racing, Ford was out as a factory. Ford's brightest minds, however, were far from finished. Holman and Moody formed a company that purchased the factory's racing stock. Holman-Moody not only formed its own team, but it also began supplying other Ford operations like the Wood Brothers, Junior Johnson, Banjo Matthews, and Bondy Long. Among the people who worked at Holman-Moody were engine builders Robert Yates, Waddell Wilson, and Jake Elder. Cale Yarborough once swept the shop's floors. "Your eyes would pop wide open when you walked into the Holman-Moody shop," Johnson once said. "It was like a huge candy shop. Give me one of those and two of these. Engines, trannies by the dozens."

Although Ford won races, it was not until 1963 that the Company won a title. And it won two: the Wood Brothers winning the car owner's championship and Weatherly taking the driver's title after the Bud Moore team made a late-season switch to Mercury. Two years later, Ned Jarrett won the title in what was Ford's most successful season to date: Jarrett won thirteen races driving Bondy Long's Ford.

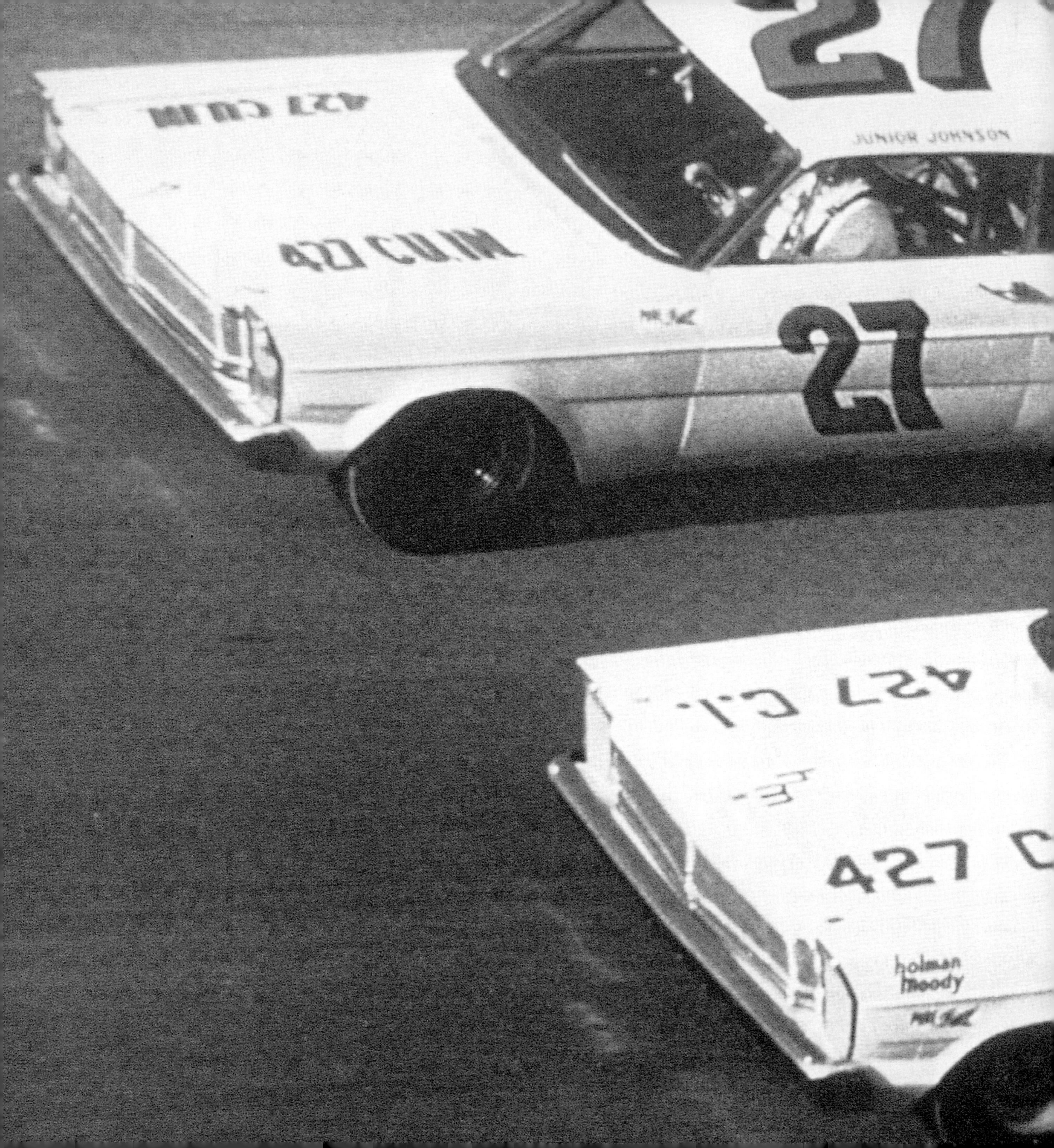
427 CU IN
JUNIOR JOHNSON
27
427 C.I.
holman
moody

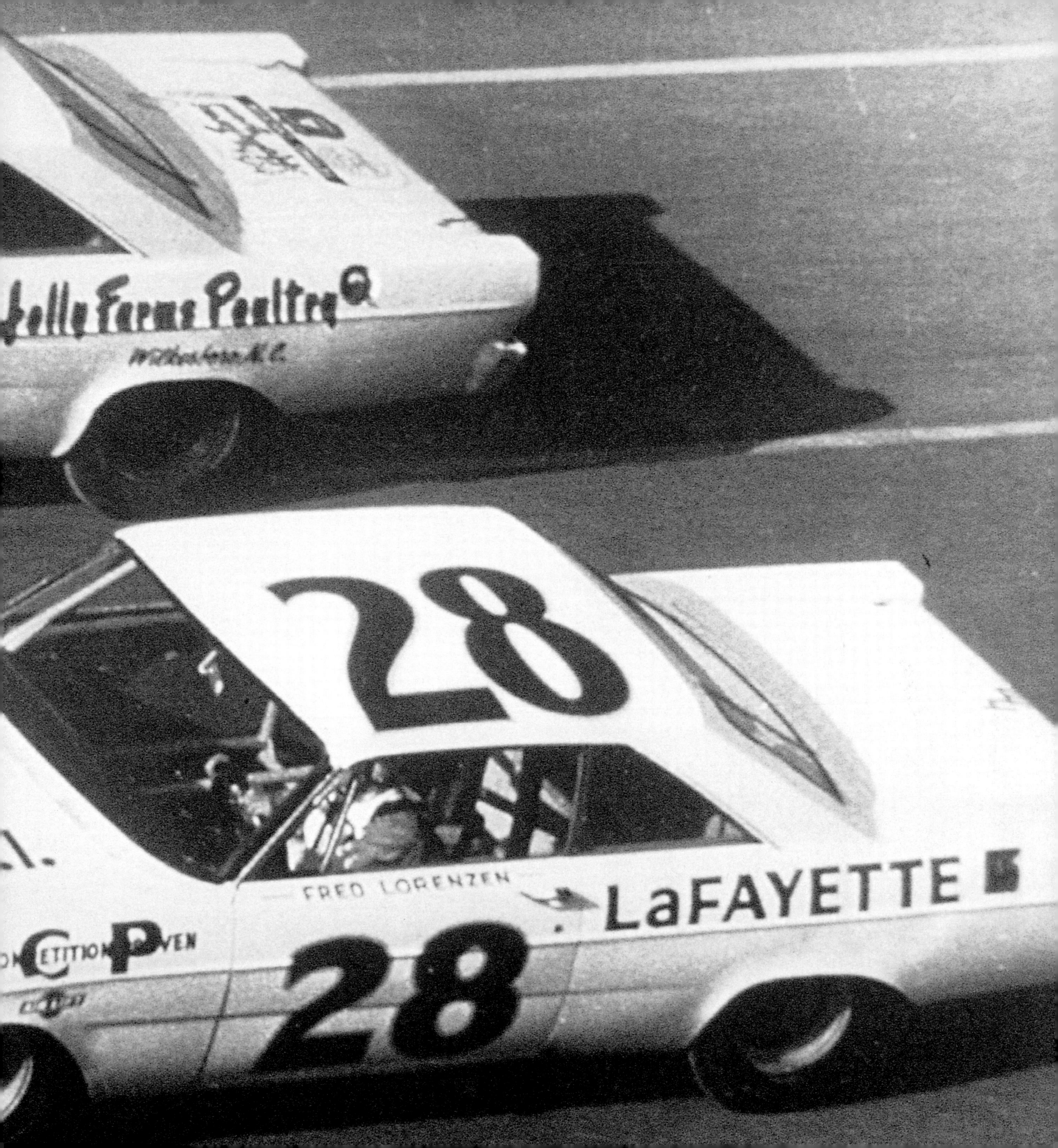
Farms Poultry
28
FRED LORENZEN
LaFAYETTE
28

Junior Johnson also won thirteen races for Ford. During the course of the season, Fords won forty-nine of the fifty-five races.

The most feared Ford driver was David Pearson—first in the Holman-Moody Ford and later in the Wood Brothers' Mercury. Pearson won twenty-seven races and back-to-back NASCAR Winston Cup Series titles for Holman-Moody in 1968–69—the only two years Pearson campaigned a full schedule. The 1969 season was particularly eventful for Ford beginning with the Daytona 500, which saw the first of the "aerodynamic" Fords. Pearson claimed the pole for Holman-Moody with the first 190-mph lap ever (190.029), and LeeRoy Yarborough won the race for Junior Johnson. Even Richard Petty drove a Ford in 1969. Pearson won a total of thirty races for Holman-Moody and forty-three more for the Wood Brothers from 1972 to 1979—a total of seventy-three wins, by far the most for a single Ford driver.

By the late 1970s, Ford had replaced its Fairlane and Torino lines and the Mercury Cyclone in the NASCAR Winston Cup Series with a single model—the Ford Thunderbird. The Thunderbird first appeared in 1978. Driving for Bud Moore, Bobby Allison scored the first thirteen wins for the Thunderbird from 1978 through the end of the 1980 season. Twenty-three of the first twenty-four Thunderbird wins posted by Fords were owned by Moore or the Wood Brothers. Then, on November 20, 1983, on the road course at Riverside, California, Bill Elliott won his first race in a Thunderbird owned by Harry Melling. Elliott would go on to be the driver with the most wins of the two-decade Thunderbird era and one of the greatest superspeedway drivers ever in the NASCAR Winston Cup Series.

In 1985, Elliott won a single-season record—eleven superspeedway races—in his Thunderbird. The count included the Daytona 500, the Winston 500 at Talladega, and the Southern 500 at Darlington, giving Elliott the Winston Million for winning three of NASCAR's four "crown jewel" races. Two years later, Elliott's Thunderbird posted the fastest qualifying lap in NASCAR history (212.809 mph at Talladega), and in 1988 he captured the NASCAR Winston Cup Series championship. Elliott claimed 40 of the 184 wins posted by Ford drivers during the Thunderbird era.

In 1992, Ford doubled with Alan Kulwicki to win the driver's title and Ford's first manufacturer's championship of the modern era. Elliott and Davey Allison both won five races, with Ford claiming sixteen of the twenty-eight events. In 1994, led by Rusty Wallace's eight wins and runner-up finish in the NASCAR Winston Cup Series race, Ford won its second manufacturer's championship in three years.

"It was sad for me to see that Thunderbird nameplate go away," said Elliott. "But we turned a new page with the Taurus"—and raced toward the twenty-first century.

David Pearson's most famous win for Ford was in the fabled 1976 Daytona 500. Pearson won a record seventy-three races for the Ford Motor Company—forty-four in Mercurys and twenty-nine in Fords. This run with Ford began with back-to-back NASCAR Grand National championships in 1968–69 for the powerful Holman-Moody Ford team. He later drove Mercurys for the Wood Brothers.

Bill Elliott (9) was the winningest driver of Ford's Thunderbird era. "Awesome Bill from Dawsonville," Georgia, won a record forty races in the Thunderbird model. His 1985 season was unprecedented in NASCAR history. In addition to winning the Winston Million by winning three of NASCAR's "crown jewel" races—the Daytona 500, Winston 500 (Talladega) and Southern 500 (Darlington)—Elliott set an all-time record with eleven wins in superspeedway races, including six from the pole. Elliott also won the NASCAR Winston Cup championship in 1988.

FORD IN RACING

Like the Ford Taurus? Well, get ready for a change.

Although the four-door Taurus was successful beyond expectations in its first two seasons of racing on NASCAR's Winston Cup Series, Ford engineers and technicians have developed a "new" Taurus for the 2000 campaign.

Building on success is nothing new for Ford's NASCAR programs. The classic Ford Thunderbird, which won 184 races in its two-decade run, was modified at least three times as Ford sought to improve upon a proven winner.

Fords have been at the forefront of stock car racing since before NASCAR was formed in 1948. Ford's flathead V-8 and pre-World War II coupes were the backbone of early stock car and modified racing. But the introduction of NASCAR's Strictly Stock Division—the forerunner of the NASCAR Winston Cup Series—in 1949 forced drivers to look in new directions.

Because the Ford factory wasn't involved in NASCAR until 1955, the drivers who picked Ford products did so for a specific reason. With most of NASCAR's formative races being run on dirt ovals, drivers opted for large, sturdy cars that could take a beating. Ford enthusiasts typically opted for the Lincoln Club Coupe and Mercury Monterey models as well as the four-door sport sedans. Jim Roper won NASCAR's first Strictly Stock race on June 19, 1949, in a Lincoln on the rutted dirt oval at the Charlotte, North Carolina Speedway.

Through 1955, Ford products won only eleven races and the Ford line scored only three of those wins. When the Ford factory officially got involved with stock car racing in 1955, the company looked at engines as well as body design. Both a more powerful V-8 and a streamlined Fairlane evolved.

Ford totally redesigned its model line for 1955 with the sleeker Fairlane replacing the boxier Mainline and Crestline models. And under the hood was a new and larger overhead valve V-8.

On the track, Ford's big push into stock car racing came in the 1956 season and was a two-pronged effort. In the Grand National Division, Ford ran the Ford Fairlane and the Mercury Monterey. And in NASCAR's new Convertible Division, Ford dominated with the Fairlane Sunliner. By the end of the fifties, the Ford Thunderbird had replaced the Mercurys on the NASCAR Grand National Series. Ford continued to refine its line in the 1960s with the more streamlined LTD and Galaxie lines.

But it was the introduction of the fastback Ford Torino and Mercury Cyclone lines in 1968 that brought an entirely new word into stock car racing . . . aerodynamics.

The factory's stock skyrocketed with the new cars. David Pearson won sixteen races and the NASCAR Grand National championship in 1968 in a Torino prepared by the Holman-Moody team. He won eleven more races and a second title in 1969. Over the two seasons, Fords and Mercurys won a total of fifty-seven races. The list of Torino drivers included Richard Petty.

By 1972, Ford had shifted its stock car teams into the Mercury Montego hardtop, which remained the factory's staple until the introduction of the Ford Thunderbird in 1978.

From 1978 until the introduction of the Taurus in 1998, the Thunderbird line would win 184 races for twenty-two drivers at twenty-three different tracks for thirteen teams.

The decision to replace the Thunderbird after the 1997 season was seen as risky. Thunderbirds had won eighteen races in 1997, the model's second-most wins after the twenty-win season of 1994. But the Taurus quickly made believers of friend and foe—winning fifteen races in its introductory season. That was more wins than the Thunderbird line had won in its first five seasons.

Taurus drivers pushed their way to the top of the points standings early in the 1999 season while contemplating what the next season would bring with the arrival of the new 2000 Taurus.

The first vision of America's favorite family car and America's fastest race car, the Ford Taurus—belonged to Don Miller.

Co-owner and general manager of Penske Racing South, the Mooresville, North Carolina, racing operation that fields fast Fords for former NASCAR Winston Cup Series champion Rusty Wallace, Miller was the point man in what proved to be one of the most remarkable stories in the history of American motorsports.

Miller and his coworkers at Penske Racing South gave the Taurus its first life as a race car. The job they started in January 1997 ended thirteen months later with a strong fleet of Tauruses filling the high banks of Daytona International Speedway as the 1998 NASCAR Winston Cup Series season began. By season's end and into the 1999 schedule, the impact of the Taurus would be felt from coast to coast and from short-track to sweeping superspeedway as Ford teams put their drive and desire to win to formidable tests, coming through in bullish fashion.

In 1998, the Taurus, a virtually unknown racing commodity at the dawn of the season in February, scored big numbers. Ford drivers won fifteen races and led 59 percent of the laps run, and Ford teams finished in four of the top five positions in the NASCAR Winston Cup Series point standings. The Taurus was at the front all season, scoring 100 top-five finish positions of a possible 165, easily leading the circuit in that category. That strength carried over into 1999.

There is a temptation to say the Taurus is simply a great race car and that its performance in its first season in the world's most competitive stock car racing series was a matter of course, a deed to be expected. But that would be too simple.

The NASCAR Winston Cup Series Taurus is a marvel of engineering, construction, teamwork, and devotion. Its development is a story of some of auto racing's best engineers, designers, team owners, and drivers coming together to create one of motorsports' most stirring successes.

The result of one of the most concentrated design efforts in car racing history was the striking red-white-and-blue Ford Taurus, opposite, unveiled at the Indiana Convention Center on July 30, 1997.

Development
From Street to Speedway

Perhaps more surprising than the Taurus's big run through NASCAR Winston Cup Series racing in 1998 and 1999 is the fact that it arrived on time and in full battle dress. For the Taurus, in most circles, was expected to become a player in NASCAR racing for the first time in 1999, not in the sport's 50th anniversary year of 1998.

Ford's acceleration of the Taurus project began in late January 1997 when company officials decided to discontinue production of the Thunderbird, the Ford model used in NASCAR Winston Cup Series racing, at the end of the 1997 model year. Talk of racing the Taurus was already far beyond the tentative stages; now the Taurus development system had to be supercharged.

The official announcement of the Thunderbird production decision came in March 1997. Nowhere was it met with more interest than at Penske Racing South, where Miller and other officials had reached an agreement only two months earlier to serve as the lead development team for the Taurus project.

"It was like a bolt out of the blue," said Miller. "The wick got turned up. We had said, 'Well, we'll be able to do this easily in a year.' We had started work, and I had done some rough sketches of what the car might look like and given them to Ford. That's the point when Bruce Cambern, then director of Special Vehicle Operations, Ford's motorsports arm, called and said, 'I've got some good news and some bad news. The good is that we want you to go ahead with the development; the bad is that we need it in July instead of a year from now.'"

Penske Racing South, one of the most watched teams in NASCAR Winston Cup Series racing, was in the process of beginning a busy racing season and had more than a full plate of competition problems to consider. Now the accelerated development of the Taurus was added to the mix.

"I said, 'Oh, boy,' Miller recalls. 'This is real cool.' There was a point there where we were confronted with sheer panic."

But Miller and his associates took the challenge, putting more and more time and more and more emphasis into the Taurus project. They began with a simple directive from NASCAR: the car body had to be built to sit on the Thunderbird chassis, one then in use in NASCAR Winston Cup Series racing, so no new chassis development would be needed.

Dec. 6 ... Discussions started about replacing the Thunderbird with the Taurus.

Day 1
Jan. 27 ... First Taurus concept meeting took place at Ford Special Vehicle Operations.

Day 5
Jan. 31 ... Taurus launch date advanced to February 1998.

During the first meeting about developing the Taurus for NASCAR Winston Cup Series racing, Penske Racing South co-owner and general manager Don Miller started drawing his vision of the racing Taurus on a sheet of paper. A commercial artist earlier in his life, Miller's concept was remarkably close to the final product.

D. MILLER

During the development of the Taurus, a number of artists drew their ideas for the car's final appearance. The drawing of the 1998 car was a Ford Motor Company concept. The drawing of the No. 2 Taurus was penned by Penske Racing South general manager Don Miller as the preliminary idea for the actual paint scheme used on Rusty Wallace's car.

WHEELS

The first 40-percent model of the Taurus awaited two days of wind tunnel testing at Southampton, England. The first tests were conducted on April 4–5, 1997, and included the Thunderbird design. The Taurus was shown to have 140 pounds more downforce than the Thunderbird.

Day 12
Feb. 7 ... First clay model of standard Ford Taurus delivered to Penske Racing South.

Day 15
Feb. 10 ... Work started on 40-percent model of Taurus race car.

Day 34
March 1 ... First 40-percent Taurus racing model completed using NASCAR dimensional criteria.

Day 48
March 15 ... Ford announced Thunderbird model would be discontinued at end of 1997 year.

A foam film was spread across the Taurus model prior to each wind tunnel test in England. During the test, the force of the wind pushed the foam across the body form, showing the exact path of the wind. The wind tunnel tests simulated speeds from 150 to 200 mph.

There was input from Ford's Special Vehicle Operations personnel and Ford's Motorsport Technology Group. Steadily, the Taurus grew from a phantom race car on the pages of Miller's sketch pads to a four-tenths-scale model to a for-real race vehicle. In the Penske shop, engineer Andy Scriver and mechanics Max Crawford and Ralph Brawley took charge of the development, working to produce a Taurus-like model that could undergo the first critical tests of the venture.

Ford engineer Preston Miller, a wise veteran of NASCAR garage areas and a key figure in much of Ford's stock car success over the years, checked in with advice and comment. "We had a good perception of what the end result might be because of the way NASCAR had approached the development of other new cars," Miller said. "We worked with comparable heights and lengths and worked within what we thought NASCAR would expect from the overall packaging. It was a sort of connect-the-dots idea based on the criteria NASCAR had set up for previous models."

The first result was the four-tenths-scale model. It looked good on the floor of the Penske shop, but how would its shape fare in racing conditions? The Taurus development team turned to a favorite tool—the wind tunnel.

The Taurus scale model was shipped to Southampton, England, to a wind tunnel facility the Penske group had used on several occasions. The tunnel creates race-like conditions, sending waves of wind slicing over, under, and beside the car to provide a realistic picture of how it will react on a high-speed racing surface.

The results in England were promising. Several body modifications followed, and the model was tested by wind tunnel technology again, this time in a facility in California. Penske had gone east and west in search of answers.

Day 57
March 24 ... First molds completed for wind tunnel testing.

Day 60
March 27 ... First model shipped to England for wind tunnel testing.

Days 68–69
April 4–5 ... During two-day tests at Southampton University, Taurus model No. 1 was tested along with Thunderbird.

By April, sheet metal fabricators in the Penske shop, one of the most advanced in NASCAR racing, had joined the team. Working under the direction of engineer David Little, the team put together the first true race Taurus. Penske crew chief Robin Pemberton was balancing new-car development with the hard reality of racing the NASCAR Winston Cup Series in real time.

"We worked on it every opportunity that we weren't working on a Thunderbird," Pemberton said of the Taurus. "The plan was to race first and worry about the Taurus second, but we knew we had an obligation to Ford."

On May 14, 1997, Penske presented the car to other Ford teams and NASCAR officials in a meeting at the Penske Racing South shop. For the first time, Ford team owners, mechanics, and drivers got a close look at the car they would be racing in only nine months. None had made any significant start on Taurus production in their shops, mainly because they were awaiting the results of the development work at Penske and NASCAR's reaction to it.

NASCAR's response to the May 14 version of the car was not good. The car looked slick and snappy—too snappy. Officials wanted some changes in the body configuration, something to make the car "less slick."

"The key at that point was that NASCAR decided it had better get involved," said Dan Davis, who would follow Cambern into the racing hot seat at Ford in November, joining the Taurus project midstream. "They knew we were under a time crunch and that we couldn't go back and forth with them about changes. They got actively involved in making sure the time frame we had could be met."

Still, there were delays. Ford initially hoped to show its new race car to the public on July 4 in conjunction with the holiday race at Daytona Beach, Florida, but circumstances pushed the unveiling to later that month.

The front end of the Taurus was still being modified when the first prototype was being fabricated at the Penske Racing South shop in Mooresville, North Carolina.

Day 108
May 14 ... First full-size mockup shown to Ford teams and NASCAR officials for the first time at Penske Racing South.

May 14 ... NASCAR technical director Gary Nelson requested changes to low roof line.

Day 109
May 15 ... Penske Racing South given go-ahead to build second 40-percent model.

Day 114
May 20 ... Second 40-percent model of Taurus completed.

Still in the early stages of
construction, the first Taurus prototype,
below, built at Penske Racing South
became the Taurus.

To reduce weight, the 40-percent model, left, used for rolling road wind tunnel tests at Southampton, England, and at San Clemente, California, was constructed of carbon fiber composite materials.

Below, Ford originally requested a model with a Sundercut nose to make the racing Taurus look like the passenger model. The indented nose didn't help the problems encountered in reducing wind drag.

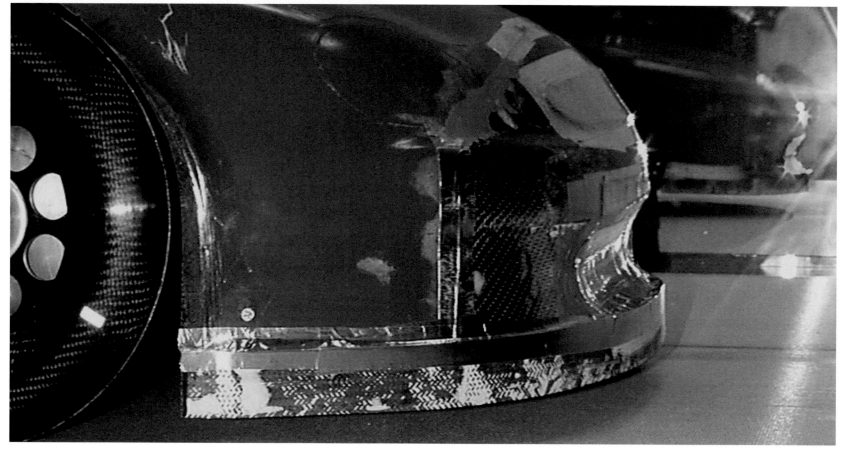

Day 124
May 30 ... Wind tunnel tests on Thunderbird and Taurus models No. 1 and No. 2 began at Swift Engineering in San Clemente, California.

Day 127
June 2 ... Forty-percent clay model of Chevy Monte Carlo produced to be used as a comparison in future Taurus wind tunnel tests.

Day 145
June 20 ... Nose and tail molds from full-sized Penske Taurus sent to Roush Racing for use in building full-sized Taurus.

Day 154
June 29 ... First wind tunnel test of full-size prototype at Lockheed-Martin in Marietta, Georgia.

As fabricators at Penske Racing South completed the work on the second MK2 prototype, a third frame was being prepared to receive body panels.

Day 164
July 9 ... NASCAR's Gary Nelson visited Penske Racing South to review latest Taurus modifications.

Day 170
July 15 ... Taurus model No. 2 updated for further wind tunnel tests at Swift.

Day 171
July 16 ... Taurus race car production begun by Ford's NASCAR Winston Cup teams.

Two areas of emphasis for the design team were the nose and roof of the Taurus. Below, a Penske Racing South engineer made final revisions to the nose. At right, workers checked the level of the roof after NASCAR requested modifications to raise the roof to match the height of other NASCAR Winston Cup Series models.

After all the modifications were completed, the Taurus MK1 was sent to the body and paint shop at Penske Racing South on July 7, 1997. A week later, the brilliant red-white-and-blue Taurus was ready for the finishing touches, which included electrical wiring, glass, suspension adjustments, and decals.

Day 180
July 25 ... Penske Racing South completed full-sized Taurus for first public display.

Days 182–183
July 27–28 ... Wind tunnel tests were held at Swift with Taurus No. 2, Thunderbird, and Chevy Monte Carlo.

Workers at Penske put the finishing touches on the first race-ready Taurus on July 25, 1997, and the car was shipped to Indianapolis, where the world would get its first look at Ford's future in stock car racing during preparations for the Brickyard 400 at Indianapolis Motor Speedway. On July 30, a crowd of more than three hundred, including news media, team representatives, and eighteen Ford drivers, gathered at the Indiana Convention Center for the car's unveiling.

Curtains parted and fog filled the front of the room, and the red-white-and-blue car emerged from darkness, Ford drivers encircling it. Although many refinements remained to be made before the car would be raced in competition half a year later, the first big hurdle had been cleared.

"At that point, that literally was the only Taurus that existed," Davis said.

That was a fact that Ford's NASCAR Winston Cup Series teams knew all too well. In the middle of a bustling racing season, they faced a daunting task to build new Tauruses to test and refine while trying to keep their current Thunderbirds strong and competitive. After Indianapolis, work accelerated in shops throughout the Ford family.

Day 185
July 30 ... Taurus race car unveiled to media and public for first time at Indiana Convention Center, Indianapolis.

The MK1 Taurus prototype, left, developed for the NASCAR Winston Cup Series sat next to the passenger Taurus.

Right, looking into the carburetor-powered Ford Taurus V-8 NASCAR engine.

Below, Ford's cadre of drivers, led by Rusty Wallace (left) and Dale Jarrett (at the nose of the car), were on hand for the Taurus coming-out party on July 30, 1997, at the Indiana Convention Center, Indianapolis.

Events began to happen quickly.

On September 2, 1997, the Taurus—it was once again the very busy car that had been born at Penske and shown at Indy—made its debut on a NASCAR track in test runs at the Daytona International Speedway in Florida. The test pilots were Rusty Wallace and Bill Elliott. Wallace was the first to drive the car at speed.

The first Taurus was built as a developmental car to run at the Indy debut so it was built with a high quarter panel. "They didn't generate great lap times, and we didn't expect them to," said Preston Miller. "We knew the drag numbers on the car were high for Daytona. But we think the test got a pretty good political spin in terms of being optimistic."

Wind tunnel tests had given Ford's movers and shakers strong evidence that the Taurus, with its rounded design, could be in trouble at Daytona and Talladega, NASCAR's two fastest tracks. At lap speeds approaching 200 mph, a race car's shape is a major factor in how fast it can be driven, primarily because its shape impacts how the rushing wind moves along its sides and over its roof. Engineers realized quickly that the unique design of the Taurus, one that made it attractive to a large segment of the American car market, gave it a difficult ride at Daytona. The car's rounded shape funneled air almost directly to the spoiler—an aluminum strip mounted on the back of the rear deck— and that thrust of air provided excessive downforce and increased drag.

So the Daytona test ended with tempered optimism. Ford knew it had a good race car, but there was concern about the Taurus's ability to fight the wind at Daytona and Talladega. More specified track testing was needed.

Back in Ford shops around the circuit, the work continued. Teams toiled into the night at many locations, facing both the important final weeks of the 1997 season and the promise of the season to come. Work was slowed by uncertainty over the final form the Taurus would take and, as a result, probably less than 10 percent of the cars needed to open the 1998 season were completed as the calendar turned to December.

Then came one of the biggest weeks in the Taurus development story. NASCAR and Ford scheduled a three-day test at Talladega Superspeedway in Alabama on December 16–18 to take a long, hard look at the car's status under high-speed conditions. When the teams arrived at the giant 2.66-mile track, enough testing had been done to make two things obvious: the Taurus faced difficulty at the tour's two superfast tracks, and it was going to be a terrific race car at the middle-range and shorter tracks. Those realities created an interesting scenario as teams wrestled with their brand-new cars.

Day 186
July 31 ... Full-sized Taurus shipped to Detroit for scanning to produce new 40-percent model and reference templates.

Day 192
August 6 ... Detroit meeting held to schedule final wind tunnel tests and first track tests. Approval given for third wind tunnel test model.

Day 219
Sept. 2 ... Rusty Wallace and Bill Elliott drove prototype in first track tests at Daytona International Speedway.

Key team owners Robert Yates and Jack Roush entered—and left—the Talladega test with different opinions about the future. Both knew the Taurus probably would be strong on shorter tracks. Yates, however, was very concerned about performance at Daytona and Talladega and thought Ford teams should push for concessions from NASCAR to give the Taurus more of a fighting chance in the four races—all among the most important of the season—at those tracks. But Roush felt changes could take away from the strength he anticipated at middle-range and shorter tracks, which make up the vast majority of the schedule.

Tossed into the mix was what Dan Davis called a potpourri of cars as teams used different interpretations of NASCAR concepts to construct the Taurus models they brought to Talladega. "All of a sudden you had all the teams building their versions of the car, and they were all different," said Davis. "Everybody's interpretation of how to build the car to fit NASCAR templates was open to discussion."

The test also marked the first time that Ford officials and teams had been able to see how the car performed in a group of Tauruses, a particularly critical element for success on the big tracks.

Jimmy Spencer led the test runs with a speed of 190.723 mph. Dale Jarrett and Michael Waltrip also broke the 190-mph barrier.

"All kinds of machinations were going on about nose height, hood height, rear deck height," Davis said. "And we were sharing every piece of information that was gathered with NASCAR. We didn't know how the car was going to be, and NASCAR didn't either. They sat in on the end-of-day briefings with all the teams. And all the teams worked together. It wasn't a time for one team to hide data and knowledge from the others. We were all in this kettle together."

To compare notes, members of the Penske team virtually rebuilt a car overnight in the Talladega garage so data could be acquired from a different perspective the following day.

Davis said the teams left Talladega with Yates and Roush "having a true difference of opinion" as to the relative strength of the Taurus at the large superspeedways. Another test was scheduled at Lowe's Motor Speedway two days later to gather more information.

The Charlotte experience was a bell-ringer. As most mechanics had predicted, the Taurus was a huge hit on the 1.5-mile track, its configuration providing excellent downforce qualities and allowing the car to "stick" to the track surface through the turns—an almost ideal situation.

"Everybody was totally elated at Charlotte about how much better the car felt," Preston Miller said. "It was a much better car in terms of aerodynamic smoothness. The nose was much rounder than the Thunderbird's, so the nose could change direction in the air without much resistance. And it

Days 223–225
Sept. 6–8 ... The third Taurus model produced drag coefficients that were very close to updated Thunderbird and Monte Carlo models during wind tunnel tests at Swift.

Days 276–279
Oct. 29–Nov. 1 ... The fourth wind tunnel test at Swift concentrated on reducing areas of drag.

Day 313
Dec. 5 ... Track testing began at Homestead, Florida. Teams agreed to go forward with design produced by Penske Racing South.

was a lot more stable than the Thunderbird. Everybody was so happy with what they had there. They were ecstatic."

The work of numerous Ford teams had paid off.

"Todd Parrott [the Dale Jarrett team crew chief] and Robert Yates probably did the most development on the car after Penske Racing finished the Taurus," said Rusty Wallace. "We were contracted to build the Taurus and have it at the unveiling in Indianapolis, and we did that. That was a pretty rushed deal, and Don Miller and our guys did a pretty good job with it. And the Ford officials were there every step of the way."

Looming on the horizon, though, was Daytona, and the biggest race of the season—the Daytona 500. The Taurus would debut in the most important stock car event of the year, and concern over the model's performance in tests at Daytona remained a difficult matter as overworked Ford teams took a short holiday vacation.

The new calendar year opened with a pair of Ford tests at Daytona. There was room for optimism as teams showed minor speed gains, mostly the result of hour after hour of intense off-season work in shops as crew chiefs and mechanics tried to milk every ounce of power from their new ride. Rookie Kenny Irwin led all drivers in the Daytona tests, pushing a Taurus to a speed of 190.609 mph. Thunderbird aerodynamic tricks did not work on Taurus cars. It was a new breed of champion in the making.

"Teams worked on making improvements in the chassis and on how to get the car lower to the ground with shock development, and all that helped," Preston Miller said. "We started seeing improved times. And the car was a little more stable. But we still had the drag discrepancy we had identified in the very first wind tunnel test. We knew we had that to wrestle with. Everyone but the Penske crew who had perceived it with the original shapes refined in hours of tunnel testing—the first Taurus was to be the best."

On February 8, in front of a huge crowd at Daytona International Speedway and with a national television audience watching, the Taurus, for months the object of intense speculation in the motorsports community, had its coming-out party. The event was the Bud Shootout, a short sprint race for pole position winners from the previous season. The Shootout wasn't a points race and provided only a brief preview of what might be expected in the Daytona 500, but it finally put the Taurus on asphalt against its competitors.

And good things happened.

In a moment of glory that completed the circle for the Penske Racing South organization, which had started the car on its rushed run months before, Rusty Wallace swept under the checkered flag

---

Days 324–326
Dec. 16–18 ... Three days of high-speed testing at Talladega Superspeedway in Talladega, Alabama. Jimmy Spencer topped the charts at 190.723 mph.

Day 328
Dec. 20 ... One day of testing at Lowe's Motor Speedway, 1997.

Days 352–354
Jan. 13–15 ... Tests at Daytona International Speedway. Kenny Irwin topped the charts at 190.609 mph.

first at the end of the Shootout, giving the Taurus a victory ride in its first competitive run. It was an electrifying result few could have anticipated only a few months before.

"It was awesome, like seeing a child born," said Don Miller. "You start with an absolutely plain sheet of paper and within six months you're sitting there with a live, fire-breathing race car."

The first chapter of the Ford Taurus story ended simultaneously with the opening of the second chapter on February 8, 1998, at Daytona International Speedway. The development of the Taurus resulted in Rusty Wallace's victory in the Bud Shootout—the car's first race and the beginning of the Taurus racing legacy.

The Taurus would roar many other times over the long run of the 1998 season, and beyond. Don Miller, who had sketched the car on a paper pad; the many engineers and mechanics who had fine-tuned it; and the drivers who had made countless test laps to perfect its power could look back at a job well done.

"The people at Penske, Roush Racing, and Robert Yates Racing—I think everybody worked together extremely well there and brought forth a great race car," said driver Dale Jarrett. "Everyone at Ford Motor Company put in their people, and they put in time and effort to make this a good race car for us. It was a tremendous effort, and I think all the Ford teams are to be commended for what they did."

The Taurus, the first four-door sedan to be raced full time in NASCAR competition, had grown from concept to reality to winner. And in record time.

The calendar read 261 days from prototype to racer.

"I think that sends a message about the character of our teams," Preston Miller said. "You can spend a lot of time agonizing over something, but when you know you have to do something, just go do it. And that's what they did."

Day 378
Feb. 8 ... Rusty Wallace
won the Bud Shootout in
the Taurus racing debut.

Clouds rolled in from the nearby Atlantic Ocean on the morning of February 6, 1998, as Rusty Wallace and the Penske Racing South team joined the line of NASCAR Winston Cup Series competitors checking in at Daytona International Speedway for Daytona 500 preparations.

It was less than a year since Ford's NASCAR Winston Cup Series teams had received the final word that the Taurus, Ford's best-selling four-door sedan, would be the car of choice for NASCAR Ford drivers in the 1998 season. As Wallace rode through the famous twin tunnels leading to the Daytona infield, much about the promise of the Taurus, rushed to its final racing configuration in the busy weeks leading to the opening of the season, remained unknown.

Some of the best automotive engineers in the world had joined forces with top mechanics and drivers from Ford's front-line NASCAR teams to develop the Taurus in the record 261 days.

Its off-season tests had been promising, but much about the Taurus remained a riddle. How would it respond in high-speed traffic? How would Daytona's famous draft, in which cars race within inches of each other in long freight train–like lines, affect the car? Would its handling characteristics give drivers an edge—or a deficit—in battle with Chevrolets and Pontiacs?

Wallace and the rest of the drivers in the Ford fleet would soon have some answers. Practice for the Daytona 500 and several supporting events, including the Bud Shootout, opened on February 6, giving teams their first extended look at the cars they had chosen to race in the pressure-cooker atmosphere leading to stock car racing's biggest event.

Ford teams immediately pointed to the Shootout, scheduled for February 8, as a vehicle to provide some hard information about the status of the Taurus. Although not an official NASCAR Winston Cup Series point race, the twenty-five-lap Shootout would provide the perfect landscape for gaining new insight into the strengths of the car.

The Tauruses of Mark Martin (6) and Dale Jarrett (88), opposite, had Jeff Gordon sandwiched late in the 1998 Dura-Lube/Kmart 500 at Phoenix International Raceway. Rusty Wallace won the event—scoring the fifteenth and final win of the first Taurus season.

Triumphs
Taurus Triumphs During 1998–1999

The result was something of a dream for Ford teams. After an off-season filled with many questions and a few tentative answers, the response they got was a victory and a sweep of the first three positions in the Taurus's competitive debut.

The race was particularly pleasant for Rusty Wallace, whose team had started the development work on the Taurus. He gunned his bright blue Ford to end a caution period with one lap to go and sprinted to the finish in front of his brother, Kenny Wallace. Also in a Taurus was third-place Bill Elliott.

Rusty Wallace, aglow after his first victory in a NASCAR Winston Cup Series car at Daytona, said the Taurus drafted well. Ford engineer Preston Miller said Wallace and his team deserved the first Taurus cheers. "They put the major effort into the operation, and they shared all their information from the start," Miller said. "It's to their credit that they get to carry the flag first."

For the first time in weeks, Ford competitors got a good night's sleep. Some of the unknowns about the Taurus had been shelved. Wallace had shown it could fight—and win—under the burden of heavy pressure at Daytona.

DAYTONA INTERNATIONAL SPEEDWAY

A week later, the NASCAR Winston Cup Series field reformed for the Daytona 500, NASCAR's marquee race and the first NASCAR Winston Cup point test for the Taurus. Here, Ford teams would see

Mark Martin (6) moved past Dale Earnhardt (3) during the 1998 Daytona 500 on February 15, 1998.

their new car in action for the first time at a long distance and in the heat of battle with a major race championship on the line.

Over a long afternoon of racing, the Taurus showed impressive strength, jousting on Daytona's high banks with race leaders and filling spots in the top ten as the event raced toward a conclusion.

At day's end, the win belonged to Chevrolet driver Dale Earnhardt, who had struggled without success for two decades in NASCAR's most important race. But the potential of the

**T**aurus teammates Jeremy Mayfield (12) and Rusty Wallace (2) took the checkered flag under the caution at the 1998 Daytona 500. Mayfield finished a Ford-best third in the NASCAR Winston Cup Series debut of the Taurus. Wallace finished fifth. Behind Wallace is Ken Schrader, who finished fourth but moved over to allow the lead Fords to cross the finish line together.

Taurus had been felt. New Penske teammates Jeremy Mayfield and Rusty Wallace formed a powerful one-two drafting tandem over the closing miles and threatened to dominate the tightrope-like racing at the front. Mayfield finished third and Wallace fifth. Chad Little, Michael Waltrip, and Bill Elliott also put Fords in the top ten.

"We had it rocking and rolling all day," Wallace said. "Jeremy and I worked like clockwork. I'm looking forward to us having a lot more races like that this year."

Ford teams left the high-stakes drama of the Daytona fortnight with one victory and another strong showing, performing much better than they might have imagined in the preceding weeks as development of the Taurus raced toward the season's opening.

NORTH CAROLINA SPEEDWAY

Next up was North Carolina Speedway, a one-mile track in the sandhills near Rockingham. The North Carolina Speedway is everything that Daytona is not—short and tight with limited passing lanes. The 400-mile race would give the Taurus its first test under such conditions and would provide its first run with a nonrestricted engine. (Races at Daytona and Talladega are run under significantly different engine rules.)

Off-season tests indicated that the Taurus, with its rounded shape and sleek lines, would be an excellent "downforce" car; that is, its form was an almost perfect match for the short- and medium-length speedways that make up the majority of facilities on the NASCAR Winston Cup circuit. While Ford teams guessed correctly that they would be at a disadvantage at Daytona and Talladega, they also felt confident about their chances at tracks like Rockingham, Charlotte, and Las Vegas.

And, as it turned out, with good reason. The Taurus did everything but win at Rockingham. Ford filled all positions from second through seventh, and second-place finisher Rusty Wallace led seventy-four laps—a performance good enough to boost him into first place in the NASCAR Winston Cup Series point standings. He finished 1.2 seconds behind Jeff Gordon, who made a late-race charge to take the win.

For the first time in his career, Rusty Wallace, left, had a teammate in 1998, Jeremy Mayfield. "I was cautious at first because I didn't know how it would work out," Wallace said, "but it was far better than I could have imagined." The pair were an important part of the Taurus development program. Wallace finished fourth in the final NASCAR Winston Cup Series standings and Mayfield was a career-best seventh.

Day 358
Feb. 15 ... Jeremy Mayfield ran third in Daytona 500.

Jeff Burton (99) nosed ahead of fellow Taurus driver Jeremy Mayfield (12) as both passed to the inside of seven-time NASCAR Winston Cup Series champion Dale Earnhardt during the AC Delco 400 at Rockingham, North Carolina, on November 1, 1998.

ROMP AT LAS VEGAS

Las Vegas a gamble? Not for the Taurus.

On the first day of March 1998 at the sparkling new speedway in the Nevada desert, motorsports history of an unusual sort was made. It isn't enough to say that Ford dominated the Las Vegas 400. A better verb would be decimated.

At day's end, thirteen—count 'em, thirteen—Fords were found in the top fourteen in the finish order. Nine of the first ten positions were filled by the Ford Taurus, and Ford team owner Jack Roush put all five of his cars in the top ten, an accomplishment few owners will be able to match in any motorsports series. It was quite a way to celebrate the Taurus's first NASCAR Winston Cup Series point victory—a win scored by Mark Martin.

Ford won virtually everything there was to win in the first visit to the NASCAR Winston Cup Series track. Dale Jarrett sped to the pole with a lap of 168.224 mph, and the Ford fleet seldom gave up the race-day lead. Martin's No. 6 led eighty-two laps.

Oddly enough, it appeared for a while that the win would go to anyone but Martin. His car developed a bad vibration early in the race because of a transmission problem, and he questioned whether he would be able to last four-hundred miles. So he charged to the front to lead as much as possible. The transmission smoked and sparked, but it lasted.

Jeff Burton took second, Rusty Wallace third, Johnny Benson fourth, Jeremy Mayfield fifth, Ted Musgrave sixth, Jimmy Spencer seventh, Bill Elliott ninth, and Chad Little tenth. Mayfield's effort was one of the day's highlights. He came from near the back of the field twice to finish fifth.

After the race, General Motors owners and drivers dashed to the NASCAR mobile office to protest that the Taurus was too strong, suggesting rules changes. Officials responded quickly, announcing spoiler modifications for the next race.

But Ford left Vegas with a full house.

March 1, 1998, was a banner day for Mark Martin, the Jack Roush team, and the Ford Taurus project. Martin scored the first points victory by a Taurus in the Las Vegas 400. But the bigger picture saw Tauruses score an unprecedented sweep of the top seven positions. Below, the Roush team celebrated Martin's victory. Following spread, Martin led fellow Taurus drivers Dale Jarrett and Rusty Wallace off the fourth turn early in the Las Vegas 400.

Day 399
March 1 ... Mark Martin
scored first Taurus win at
Las Vegas as Tauruses
swept first seven positions.

Fords led 312 of the race's 393 laps, including the first 198, establishing the Taurus as a force to be reckoned with on medium-range speedways.

"I told everybody at Daytona that on a scale of one to ten, the Taurus was an eight," Rusty Wallace said. "It's a really good car, but we're still working on it."

Geoffrey Bodine, who rode a Taurus home fifth, was impressed with the car's first run at a medium-length speedway. "The Taurus is going to be a great car for us," Bodine said.

If anyone needed any more proof, it came the next week—and it came in waves.

LAS VEGAS MOTOR SPEEDWAY

The NASCAR Winston Cup circuit rolled west to Las Vegas for its first race at the Las Vegas Motor Speedway, a 1.5-mile track on the outskirts of one of the hemisphere's biggest entertainment capitals. Praised by drivers for its smooth surface and wide track, the speedway attracted a sellout crowd of more than one hundred thousand to its first NASCAR Winston Cup event, and the fans saw Fords dominate on a near-perfect Taurus day.

The man of the moment was Mark Martin, a longtime Ford pilot and, on this March day, the driver who would be entered in the record books as the first to win a NASCAR Winston Cup Series point race in a Taurus. He found Las Vegas precisely to his liking and, despite lingering transmission problems, was a threat from the first green flag.

Martin ran around the Las Vegas track as if his car were attached to rails. He started in seventh place but raced in the top four most of the day, flashing his blue-and-white Taurus down the

long front straight with authority. He was particularly strong over the race's closing miles, leading fifty of the final sixty-six laps.

"We've still got a little work to do, but it's already real special," Martin said. "It's a real special win."

It was special beyond the win for Ford, which saw its emerging Taurus finish in nine of the top ten positions and in thirteen of the first fourteen while leading all but 14 of the race's 267 laps. The day was extremely productive for a car only a month out of the starting blocks. All five teams owned by Ford veteran Jack Roush finished in the top ten.

The honor of scoring the first Taurus victory on the NASCAR Winston Cup Series fell to Mark Martin in the 1998 season's third race at Las Vegas, Nevada. Three weeks earlier, Martin struggled in his debut with the Taurus, qualifying 15th and finishing 38th in the season-opening Daytona 500. But Martin rebounded in the second with a third at Rockingham, North Carolina, before leading the Taurus sweep of the top seven spots at Las Vegas.

ROUSH RACING

Take all problems and challenges associated with preparing a new model for NASCAR Winston Cup Series racing and multiply them by five. That's the challenge Jack Roush and his operation faced as the 1998 NASCAR Winston Cup Series season dawned.

Roush, one of the most respected car owners and engineers in auto racing, expanded his already impressive NASCAR Winston Cup Series operation from three to five teams for the 1998 season. Adding two teams was a big challenge, and ushering in a new car model added more complications.

"We have to build cars all year long, and, of course, we were building a bunch of race cars then," said Buddy Parrott, a veteran NASCAR mechanic and a Roush general manager. "Each one of the Roush teams has about eleven cars at their disposal, so

obviously, you're talking about quite an operation to make changes in."

The Chad Little and Johnny Benson teams joined Roush's group for 1998. Already on board were Mark Martin, Jeff Burton, and Ted Musgrave. The building process for each team was similar.

"Once we got two cars built for Daytona, we had to get two cars built for Rockingham [the second race of the year] and the next place and the next place," Parrott said. "It took a while, but with teamwork and people sticking together, and with Ford Motor Company doing all they could, we made it work.

"Penske South had done a good job getting the car designed and getting it moving. And NASCAR did a good job. They wanted to give us that car as quick as they could."

The situation at Roush Racing was helped by the remarkable

spirit of cooperation shared by the team's drivers.

"Through working together, we have gained mutual respect for each other because we're able to help each other," said Burton of his teammate Martin. "We just work well together. We're willing to help each other. When Mark Martin helps Jeff Burton, he's making it harder for himself to win the race, and we're willing to do that. That goes not only for Mark and me but with Jimmy [Fennig, Martin's crew chief] and Frank [Stoddard, Burton's crew chief]. Buddy puts it all together."

That sort of cooperation enabled Roush and his men to field practically a fleet of new race-ready Tauruses for the opening weeks of the 1998 season, meeting the sort of construction challenge that has been attempted by few motorsports operations.

The Ford sweep at Las Vegas irritated General Motors teams, leading some to express strong complaints to NASCAR officials immediately after the race. Among GM drivers, Dale Earnhardt was perhaps the most vocal. "They've only been working on it for two races, so you can imagine what it's going to be like by the time we get to Michigan and Pocono," he said of the Taurus.

NASCAR's review of the situation led to an action that Ford teams had been expecting since the start of the season—a change in rules impacting the Taurus. A day after the Las Vegas race, NASCAR announced that rear-deck spoilers on the Taurus would be trimmed one-quarter inch—a change aimed at reducing the car's downforce strength and supposedly tightening the gap between Ford and General Motors products.

ATLANTA MOTOR SPEEDWAY

The first test of the new rules would come at one of NASCAR's fastest tracks, the D-shaped Atlanta Motor Speedway in Hampton, Georgia. NASCAR Winston Cup Series teams moved from Las Vegas to Atlanta for the Primestar 500, a race originally scheduled to be run March 8 but postponed to the following day by rain.

The Taurus sparkled again in the fierce intensity of Atlanta, a difficult track that demands both high speeds and smart traffic management. Although Pontiac driver Bobby Labonte won the race, Fords finished in positions two through nine, and Kenny Irwin put a Taurus out front for 111 laps, more than any other driver.

The action in the garages begins long before the cars take to the track and continues long after the final lap is turned. Below, the crews of Rusty Wallace (2) and Bill Elliott (94) prepared their Tauruses for a final practice.

Ford's Dale Jarrett finished second and claimed that the NASCAR rules change made before the race had a negative impact on the Taurus's strength. "It made a big difference, and it was really noticeable after the tires got worn down," he said. "You had to know exactly what you were doing out there."

A major plus for the Ford contingent that day was the continued excellence shown by teammates Rusty Wallace and Jeremy Mayfield. Mayfield finished third and Wallace fourth, leaving the Penske Racing drivers one-two (Wallace first, Mayfield second) in the NASCAR Winston Cup Series point standings.

DARLINGTON RACEWAY

A week after the Atlanta race, NASCAR hit the circuit's Fords with another rules change, this time reducing the width of the Taurus's rear spoiler. That change was expected to put further limitations on the car at the next race, the TranSouth Financial 400 at Darlington Raceway (South Carolina), the tour's oldest superspeedway.

But, if the rules change was considered an obstacle, Jarrett and the Robert Yates Racing team decided to look at it as just another difficult part of an already tough assignment: beat forty-two other teams on the toughest big track on the NASCAR schedule. Darlington, famous for its oblong shape and its habit of eating race cars, presents a monster challenge on a normal race day. To enter the weekend with a car still bordering on the unknown and shackled by another rules modification produced a not-so-pretty picture.

Benefiting from late race adjustments that turned his Taurus into a rocket, Jarrett roared past leader Jeff Burton and held off charging Jeff Gordon to win the 400 by .22 of a second. The Jarrett victory illustrated the sort of can-do attitude that Taurus teams would show all season. Even when it seemed that the odds were stacked against them, they found a way to win.

Jarrett was mired in traffic much of the day, and he lost valuable track time when a dropped lug nut caused a problem in the pits. But the team's final pit stop was flawless, and Jarrett wound up in position to challenge Burton, who had dominated most of the day. With eighteen laps to go, Jarrett passed Burton to move into first place for good. Gordon's Chevrolet challenged for the win late but was no match for the No. 88 Taurus.

Ford wound up with four of the top five finishers, and Taurus drivers led every lap of the race. Quite a day for the big, blue oval at one of the most imposing speedways in racing, especially considering the continuing uncertainty over rules. Taurus driver Johnny Benson said the pre-Darlington spoiler change gave the Taurus a tough ride. "You get those things in traffic and they're a handful."

Dale Jarrett, shown below in the cockpit and at right celebrating his victory in the MBNA Platinum 400 at Dover Downs International Speedway on May 31, 1998, carried a strong third-place finish in the final 1998 NASCAR Winston Cup Series standings into a fast start for the 1999 season.

 The Penske Racing South crew
worked feverishly to keep Rusty Wallace's
Taurus ahead in the 1999 Food City 500
at Bristol, Tennessee. Wallace scored his
first win of the season from the pole.

BRISTOL MOTOR SPEEDWAY

The tour moved from Darlington, the most intimidating superspeedway, to Bristol (Tennessee) Motor Speedway, its roughest short track. The high-banked half-mile at Bristol is one of the most feared race courses in America, largely because its thirty-six-degree banking promotes astonishingly fast speeds for such a short track. Among the results—rapid packs of race cars that are bunched very closely when wrecks occur.

Acknowledging a boost from the recent rules adjustment, Chevrolet driver Jeff Gordon emerged victorious at Bristol, leading the final 63 laps. But Gordon's strength was challenged by the Taurus of Rusty Wallace, who led 220 laps before his engine trouble. Given a stronger engine, Wallace figured to be gunning for the win at the end of the day.

Ford still filled positions three through five, however, with Dale Jarrett, Jeff Burton, and Johnny Benson gaining top-five finishes.

TEXAS MOTOR SPEEDWAY

No one could have predicted the challenge the following week would bring. Next stop on the tour was Texas Motor Speedway (TMS) near Fort Worth, where Taurus teams would conquer some unusual circumstances to score another Ford victory.

Problems emerged at the 1.5-mile track when practice began Thursday. On Friday, the trouble turned major when water began seeping through the track surface, causing several cars to crash. Texas 500 qualifying was postponed from Friday to Saturday as track officials struggled to correct the problem.

Saturday's time trials produced a Taurus pole winner in Jeremy Mayfield, who ignored potential trouble spots on the track and posted a stunning qualifying speed of 185.906 mph, good enough for his second NASCAR Winston Cup Series career pole.

Water seepage problems continued, however, and Saturday's final—and most important—practice session was canceled, leaving drivers and teams with a lot of question marks leading into Sunday's race.

The Tauruses of Dale Jarrett (88) and Chad Little battled during the 1998 Texas 500 at Texas Motor Speedway. Little scored a career-best runner-up finish to Mark Martin as Fords swept the top three places on the 1.5-mile tri-oval.

It turned out, however, that the biggest problem of the day was Mark Martin. His Taurus perfectly in tune with the TMS layout, he wrestled with fellow Ford drivers Jeremy Mayfield and Jeff Burton at the front much of the day. Chad Little and Dale Jarrett also were strong in Fords.

Martin left the pits with the lead after the day's final caution and stayed in front the rest of the way. Little, in pursuit of his first NASCAR Winston Cup Series victory, shadowed Martin over the closing laps but couldn't challenge. Martin won by .57 of a second.

The Taurus again had proven its strength at medium-range tracks.

MARTINSVILLE SPEEDWAY

From Texas, the tour moved across country to the relative calm of Martinsville, Virginia, and NASCAR Winston Cup Series racing's shortest track, .526-mile Martinsville Speedway. Here, the afternoon is typically one of bumper cars, as forty-three NASCAR Winston Cup racers navigate the tight, flat track and seek tiny openings to pass. Contact is inevitable.

On this April day in Virginia, the going was particularly tough for Ford teams. A Chevrolet, the yellow No. 4 of Bobby Hamilton, was the dominant car, leading 378 of the 500 laps on the way to an easy victory.

Hamilton's Morgan–McClure Motorsports team was so close to the perfect setup for the track that few other drivers could challenge. Hamilton led all but 29 of the first 250 laps and dropped out of first place only during that period when he pitted. He was never passed for the lead on the track.

The day was a good one, however, for Taurus driver Ted Musgrave, who finished second, tying the best effort of his career. And Dale Jarrett, who has often faced struggles at Martinsville, rolled home an impressive third.

TALLADEGA SUPERSPEEDWAY

The next week, the circuit moved from the shortest track to the fastest—Talladega Superspeedway in Alabama, again bringing Ford teams face-to-face with the hurdles they

Ford Taurus drivers (from left) Robert Pressley, Jeremy Mayfield, and Mark Martin discuss strategy before the 1998 Las Vegas 400. Martin won the race to score the first NASCAR Winston Cup Series victory for the Taurus. Mayfield was fifth and Pressley finished 20th.

Rick Mast was one of thirteen Taurus drivers to finish among the top fourteen finishers in the inaugural Las Vegas 400 on March 1, 1998. Mast was one of eight Ford drivers to lead the race on the 1.5-mile tri-oval, and Dale Jarrett completed the Taurus domination by winning the pole.

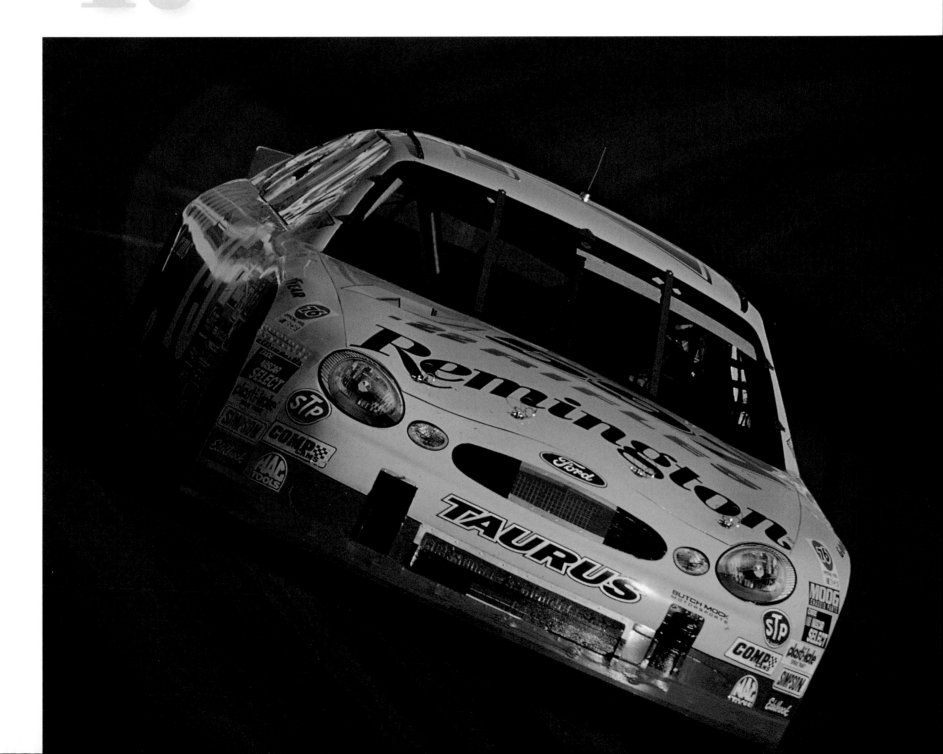

Mark Martin accepted the winner's trophy from track president Greg Penske after winning the California 500 on May 3, 1998, at California Speedway. Martin's Taurus dominated the event, leading 165 of the 250 laps around the two-mile oval. The win was the third of seven in the season for Martin, who finished second in the final NASCAR Winston Cup Series standings.

had to leap on superfast tracks. As matters developed in the DieHard 500, racing in the fast Talladega draft wouldn't be the only problem Taurus drivers would have to battle.

Race day was marred by a twenty-car incident on the Talladega frontstretch. Among those impacted was Ford driver Bill Elliott, who received a bruised sternum.

Wreckage on the frontstretch caused a red-flag delay of almost thirty minutes.

When the race restarted, Ford drivers Dale Jarrett, Kenny Wallace, and Jimmy Spencer were in the drafting line at the front and had a shot at the victory. But Pontiac driver Bobby Labonte wound up in front at the end, outgunning Spencer by .16 of a second at the finish.

Spencer said the Taurus raced with a significant handicap at Talladega. "We have a lot of drag on our race cars right now, and I think that NASCAR is going to look into that after today," he said. "I think they saw some pretty good domination by General Motors."

Jarrett called Talladega "a major traffic jam at a high rate of speed. Probably your heart rate goes up more at a place like Talladega than anywhere else as you get ready to start. You know you're going to be two and three wide all day."

CALIFORNIA SPEEDWAY

A week later, Mark Martin added more emphasis to the search for his first NASCAR Winston Cup Series championship by winning the California 500 at California Speedway in Fontana. Widely respected throughout motorsports as a racer's racer, Martin has been within shouting distance of the most coveted stock car racing title in the world several times.

At Fontana, he looked like a champion, riding a Jack Roush–owned Taurus to his third win of the season. And it wasn't close. Martin led 165 of 250 laps and coasted home more than a second in front of fellow Ford driver Jeremy Mayfield.

Normally a reserved sort, Martin was ebullient in victory lane, shouting praises for one of the best cars he had raced in years. "I tell you this car, she's awesome," he said. "She was on the money today."

The only serious threats to Martin came from Taurus drivers Mayfield and Rusty Wallace. Wallace ran second late in the day but was nailed by engine failure with twelve laps remaining. Mayfield couldn't catch Martin at the end, but his second-place finish boosted him into the NASCAR Winston Cup Series point lead.

A then career-best second-place finish in the California 500 enabled Jeremy Mayfield to climb to the top of the NASCAR Winston Cup Series standings for the first time in his career. Below, the Penske-Kranefuss crew changed two tires and refueled Mayfield during a green flag stop.

LOWE'S MOTOR SPEEDWAY

Next stop on the tour was Lowe's Motor Speedway, host in May to two of the biggest races of the season—The Winston, a non-points NASCAR all-star race and the Coca-Cola 600, the longest and one of the highest paying events of the year.

The night of the Winston is one of the most anticipated evenings of the season. The short sprint race means nothing in the chase for the NASCAR Winston Cup Series championship, but the event's large purse and rich history make it one of the highlights of the season, and every driver has eyes on its victory lane.

On this hot May night, the star would belong to Mark Martin. Martin's No. 6 Taurus roared to victory under unusual circumstances. Jeff Gordon appeared to have the win sealed, carrying the lead into the last lap of the last segment of the three-stage race. But Gordon's Chevrolet slowed entering turn one on the last lap—its fuel tank dry.

Martin's team had elected to change four tires during the race's last pit stop, and that strategy paid big dividends. When Gordon ran out of gas, the second-place Martin inherited the lead and cruised to the checkered flag first.

The Jack Roush team's four-tire pit stop had given Martin enough on-track stability to rally from sixth place to second during the race's final ten laps. When Gordon's fuel pressure dropped, Martin's heart soared. He was home free.

"I'm feeling about as lucky as anybody around, right now," Martin said after the race.

Prior to the feature race, Ford driver Jeremy Mayfield had won the The Winston Open, a fifty-lap event that qualified the winner for The Winston field.

A week after The Winston, teams returned to the business of the points championship in the Coca-Cola 600, and Ford teams again sparkled, taking five of the top ten positions. Chevrolet driver Jeff Gordon outran Rusty Wallace in the closing miles to claim the win.

DOVER DOWNS INTERNATIONAL SPEEDWAY

At Dover, Delaware, the next week, Ford returned to the front, with Jarrett scoring a win at the tight Dover Downs International Speedway. Jeff Gordon led 376 of the 400 laps, but Jarrett, helped by a key fuel-mileage decision by crew chief Todd Parrott, was in front at the finish.

RICHMOND INTERNATIONAL RACEWAY

At Richmond, Virginia, on the following Saturday night, Jarrett found himself embroiled in one of the season's biggest controversies. He finished second in the Pontiac Excitement 400 but figured he should have had first easily.

Jarrett had the lead with six laps to go when NASCAR red-flagged the race because of a four-car wreck in turn two. Without the red flag, the race probably would have ended under caution, giving Jarrett the victory. Instead, after the track cleanup, Terry Labonte

Dale Jarrett was upset after being denied victory in a controversial finish at Richmond, Virginia, on June 6, 1998. Jarrett's Taurus held the lead with six laps to go when an accident almost blocked turn two, prompting officials to throw the red flag rather than the yellow caution. Had the race finished under the yellow, Jarrett would have won. But the red flag stoppage enabled Terry Labonte to bump his way past on the final laps.

Dale Jarrett rallied from a rare poor starting position (twenty-eighth) to finish fifth in the 1999 Coca-Cola 600 at Lowe's Speedway in Charlotte, North Carolina. The comeback allowed Jarrett, shown here passing Darrell Waltrip (66), to retain his NASCAR Winston Cup Series points lead.

ROBERT YATES RACING

Robert Yates Racing approached the 1998 NASCAR Winston Cup Series season with a unique challenge.

Not only did Yates and his potent Charlotte, North Carolina-based operation—one of the most respected in auto racing—have to deal with the complexities of a new car model, but there was also a new mix on the team. Highly regarded rookie driver Kenny Irwin Jr. had joined veteran Dale Jarrett as a driver for Yates, giving the team another element to factor into what would be a complicated season.

Irwin had to learn new racetracks, new coworkers, new strategies—and a new race car. Jarrett had a new teammate and the uncertainties of the Taurus.

"I went in just thinking that I had a great team and a great car, and I still believe that," Irwin said. "I just think that this sport lends itself to experience more than anything I've ever done, . . . learning these race cars and, more than anything, learning these racetracks."

The unforgiving nature of the sport nailed Irwin at the Coca-Cola 600 at Charlotte in May as the team failed to qualify, marking the only race he missed in an adventurous season.

"You learn so much and there's so much information that you're trying to figure out that you probably forget a lot of stuff," Irwin said.

Yates, who had owned NASCAR Winston Cup racers for a decade and had a long history in the sport, admitted that all the newness of the year was overwhelming.

"The timing was terrible for our team," he said. "We had the best Thunderbirds, and we had a house full of them. We had thirty-some Thunderbirds built. But the Taurus drives well on the racetrack, and it drives well beside cars. It's fresh, it's new, and it's nice."

The year became one of triumph for Yates and his men. Jarrett won three races and finished third in the point standings. Irwin won the Rookie of the Year award and pushed to the front to lead in four races.

Driver Kenny Irwin conferred with crew chief Doug Richert during a practice before the 1999 Daytona 500. Irwin drove the Robert Yates–owned Taurus to a third.

charged to the front, bumped Jarrett out of the way two laps from the finish, and won the race. The red flag provided a more exciting finish but Jarrett was upset at the decision.

Still, the race underlined the short-track strength of the Taurus.

MICHIGAN INTERNATIONAL SPEEDWAY

In mid-June, the tour rolled into Brooklyn, Michigan, for the Miller Lite 400 at Michigan International Speedway (MIS), a track Mark Martin considers among the best in the country. And with good reason.

Martin notched his fourth win of the season at MIS, leading the final nineteen laps. "We're on a roll," Martin said. "I hope it lasts forever." It was his fifth-straight top-ten finish.

POCONO INTERNATIONAL RACEWAY

At Pocono International Raceway (PIR), the next stop, Jeremy Mayfield rode his blue-and-white Taurus to the first NASCAR Winston Cup Series victory of his career. He won the Pocono 500 on PIR's unusual triangular surface, leading 122 of 200 laps and boosting his lead in the NASCAR Winston Cup Series standings to thirty-six points.

Jeremy Mayfield's three-race run atop the NASCAR Winston Cup Series standings climaxed with the first victory of his career on June 21, 1998, on the flat, 1.5-mile track at Pennsylvania's Pocono Raceway. Mayfield's Taurus averaged 117.809 mph.

NEW HAMPSHIRE INTERNATIONAL SPEEDWAY

After Jeff Gordon won on the road course at Sonoma, California, June 28, Jeff Burton put Taurus in victory lane again at New Hampshire International Speedway July 12 with one of the best runs of his career. Burton built a lead of six seconds late in the race and led virtually all of the final 160 laps. The win was Burton's first of the year and a career first for rookie crew chief Frank Stoddard.

After the New Hampshire race, the halfway point of the year, Ford had four drivers—Mark Martin, Dale Jarrett, Jeremy Mayfield, and Rusty Wallace—in the top five in the NASCAR Winston Cup Series standings, a testimonial to the consistency of the Taurus.

After New Hampshire, Jeff Gordon went on a midseason tear, winning the next four races and tying a streak record set earlier by, among others, Ford drivers Mark Martin and Bill Elliott.

BRISTOL MOTOR SPEEDWAY

Martin ended Gordon's run on an emotional August 22 in Bristol, Tennessee, winning the Goody's Headache Powder 500. Martin dedicated the victory to the memory of his father, stepmother, and half sister, who had been killed two weeks earlier in a plane crash. "This was for them," Martin said.

Martin finished two seconds in front of teammate Jeff Burton as Ford nabbed the top four spots.

RICHMOND INTERNATIONAL RACEWAY

Gordon won the next two races—at New Hampshire and Darlington—but he ran into rapidly rising Jeff Burton at Richmond. Burton and Gordon locked horns in one of the best finishes of the season, Burton winning the Exide Batteries 400 by a hood length. The win pushed Ford's total to ten for the season.

DOVER DOWNS INTERNATIONAL SPEEDWAY

A week later, Martin was on the move again, obliterating the rest of the field in the MBNA Gold 400 at Dover, Delaware. Astonishingly, Martin led 380 of the race's 400 laps. He won by two seconds in scoring his sixth victory of the year, a career high.

Next came what was perhaps 1998's most inspirational performance.

MARTINSVILLE SPEEDWAY

Ricky Rudd entered the NAPA Autocare 500 at Martinsville needing a victory to extend his remarkable streak of winning at least once every season for sixteen years. He scored on the half-mile track, and in the worst of conditions. Temperatures soared toward the mid-nineties, and the cooling apparatus inside Rudd's car malfunctioned, turning his workplace into an oven. But his Taurus performed so well that he decided to tough out the long day, and he rolled home in first place.

Jeremy Mayfield's Taurus (12) ran ahead of Jeff Gordon early in the 1998 Pocono 500 at Long Pond, Pennsylvania.

Johnny Benson (26) went inside to pass Robert Pressley (77) in an all-Taurus battle during the 1998 Food City 500 at Bristol, Tennessee. Benson finished fifth, among his three best outings.

Ricky Rudd's victory at Martinsville, Virginia, on September, 27, 1998, is considered one of the greatest races in NASCAR history. After his personal cooling system failed, Rudd battled fatigue brought on by triple-digit temperatures throughout the 500-lap race on the .526-mile oval. He led the final ninety-six laps to claim his only victory of the season, but the win marked the sixteenth-straight year that Rudd won at least one race. Rudd and crew celebrate the continued streak in victory lane, opposite.

Rudd suffered burns on his back and received medical attention in victory lane before joining the celebration. "I had such a great car I didn't want to give it up," he said.

The Taurus baton returned to Mark Martin's hands in the next race at Charlotte. He won the UAW-GM Quality 500, showing persistence in a long day of rain delays and staying firmly in the hunt for the series championship. Martin's Taurus, showing its superiority on the 1.5-mile track, led the final sixty-six laps.

Dale Jarrett stepped to the forefront in the next race, and the timing was good. Jarrett sped to a narrow victory in the Winston 500 at Talladega, Alabama, winning a $1 million bonus as part of the R. J. Reynolds Tobacco Co.'s No Bull Five program.

Jarrett's Robert Yates Racing team, ignoring the deficit the Taurus faced on the high-speed track, gave its driver a sensational car, one strong enough to hold off a last-lap drafting charge by teammates Jeff Gordon and Terry Labonte.

"They said you couldn't win with a Taurus at those racetracks [Daytona and Talladega], and we were able to do that," Jarrett said. "It was nice to have another Ford driver there to help me. Jimmy Spencer was right on my bumper and worked very well with me."

After Jeff Gordon won the Pepsi 400 at Daytona, the spotlight returned to the Taurus at Phoenix. This time Rusty Wallace carried the colors, winning the Dura-Lube/Kmart 500 and ending a fifty-nine-race winless streak. Although the race was shortened by rain, Wallace's car was so strong that there was little chance of anyone catching him even if the event had been run to its full length. "It was like nothing I've ever had in my life," Wallace said.

**D**ale Jarrett, shown on the preceding spread leading Rusty Wallace out of a turn at California Speedway, drove his Taurus to a series of triumphs in 1998 and 1999. Crew chief Todd Parrott, left, popped the cork on the champagne and Jarrett, below, held up the $1 million check after the Robert Yates team won the Winston 500 at Talladega, Alabama, on October 11, 1998.

Jeff Gordon won the last two races of the season and took the series championship after a fierce battle with Martin, who totaled seven victories and more than enough points to win the title in most seasons. Martin finished second five times and was in the top five a remarkable twenty-two times.

Although Gordon took the championship, four Taurus drivers—in order, Martin, Jarrett, Wallace, and Burton—rounded out the top five seasonal point standings. Mayfield finished seventh. In the 1998 season, Ford totaled fifteen NASCAR Winston Cup Series victories.

The success of 1998 gave Ford teams a solid foundation for the start of the next season. Teams continued to refine the Taurus during the short off-season, looking for the extra edge that can mean the difference between first place and fifth.

By the spring of 1999, teams had made significant advances in their knowledge of and reaction to the peculiarities of the Taurus.

"You might say that the teams understand all they know now," said Preston Miller. "They knew a fair amount about the car in the first months of 1998. They just couldn't know how much more was out there with the car. They didn't understand that they might be working themselves into some corners before they got there. A year into it, they had realized that they couldn't apply all of the same logic to the building of these cars as they did to the Thunderbird."

Jarrett said year two of the Taurus offered improvement. "I think we're just a little bit better," he said. "We've got a little bit of spoiler back on the car now [thanks to a NASCAR rules change], and that has helped the downforce and the drag. But there's still a lot to be gained and a lot to be learned about the car."

The continuing strength of the Taurus was illustrated in 1999's first event—the Bud Shootout at Daytona Beach. Finishing first was Mr. Reliable—Mark Martin, who won for the first time in a stock car at Daytona. Boosted by a quick pit stop on the tenth of twenty-five laps, he rode a strong horse to the finish.

"It's hard to get cars to run as fast at Daytona as ours did today, and that's all horsepower and body work," Martin said.

The next week, Jeff Gordon won the Daytona 500 after a massive accident damaged several top Fords, including those of Martin, Dale Jarrett, Kenny Irwin, Jeff Burton, and Ricky Rudd. Irwin rallied to finish third.

Martin's potent Taurus scored again as the tour moved to Rockingham, North Carolina, the following week, with the Arkansas driver once again benefiting from a strong pit-stop effort by his team. Ford took four of the top five spots.

In race three at Las Vegas, the Taurus again showed that it virtually owns the 1.5-mile track as Jeff Burton outran his brother Ward in a late-race duel to win the Las Vegas 400. The Virginia brothers ran side by side over the closing laps, but Jeff pushed ahead to win by 1.07 seconds. He led 111 laps.

Jeff Gordon won at Atlanta the next week, but Jeff Burton made it two out of three at Darlington, edging in front late in the day and keeping his cool during an accident that started on what became the final lap. Burton was in front when rain fell, contributing to the incident and, eventually, forcing an early end to the race. He thus wound up with a dented race car but also had an important

Mark Martin gave the Taurus its second straight victory in the Bud Shootout all-star race at Daytona International Speedway on February 7, 1999.

Mark Martin (center) and two
members of the Jack Roush crew study the
Ford V-8 powerplant under the hood of
Martin's 1999 Ford Taurus.

The Ford Taurus enters the new millennium as the only model to win a NASCAR Winston Cup Series race at Las Vegas Motor Speedway, two for two. Jeff Burton (in the winner's circle below) was all smiles throughout the weekend that climaxed with his No. 99 Taurus pulling away, right. The 1998 inaugural was won by his Roush Racing teammate Mark Martin, who led a Taurus sweep of the top seven places in the field.

early-season win: he took the NASCAR Winston Cup Series point lead. "Even if the rain hadn't happened, we had the best car today," he said.

Although a Taurus would win only one of the next five races after Darlington, consistent top-five efforts by Burton, Jarrett, and Martin carried them to the top of the points race. Jarrett finished second to native Texan Terry Labonte in the Primestar 500 at Texas Motor Speedway on March 28. Two weeks later, on the half-mile oval at Bristol, Tennessee, Rusty Wallace led a 1-2-3 Taurus sweep, with Martin finishing second, Jarrett third, and Burton fifth. Burton retained his points lead while Jarrett, who had moved steadily forward in the standings ever since finishing thirty-sixth in the season-opening Daytona 500, climbed into second.

On April 18, Burton protected his lead by finishing second in the Goody's Body Pain 500 on the short track at Martinsville, Virginia. But Jarrett, who was a solid eighth in Martinsville, regained his momentum when the tour returned to the longer ovals.

Jarrett's sprint to the top of the standings began with his runner-up finish to Earnhardt in the DieHard 500, where Martin came in third. A week later, Burton ran second to Gordon at California Speedway, where Jarrett was fifth.

The breakthrough for Jarrett came on May 15 at Richmond, Virginia, where he won his first race of the season and climbed past Burton into the points lead. "Everybody kept saying, 'When are you going to win?' Jarrett said. "I guess we were just biding our time." Jarrett claimed the nineteenth victory of his career despite starting from the twenty-first spot on the grid. In his only previous win at Richmond, Jarrett had started twenty-third.

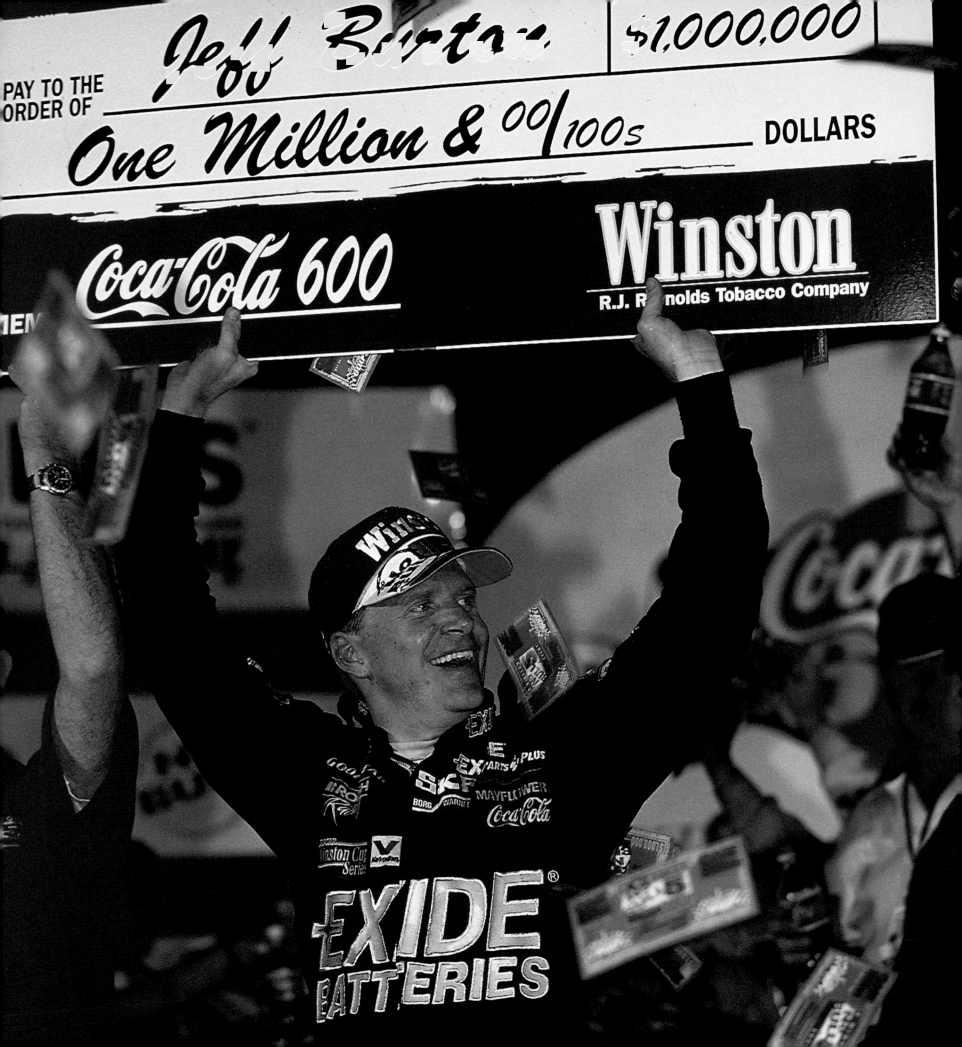

Victory Lane celebrations increased for the Ford Taurus teams in 1999. Left, Jeff Burton celebrated winning the No Bull Million supplement to his triumph in the Coca-Cola 600 at Lowe's Motor Speedway in Charlotte, North Carolina. Below, the entire Penske Racing South team joined winning driver Rusty Wallace (center, with fist pumped in the air) after the April 11 Food City 500 at Bristol, Tennessee.

"Maybe the key for us is to start far back and work forward," said Jarrett, who quickly turned his thoughts toward the NASCAR Winston Cup championship race. "We're going to go after this championship," Jarrett said, "and we didn't want to be the champion without a victory."

Burton was leading midway through the race when transmission problems dropped him to thirty-seventh. He rallied two weeks later by winning the Coca-Cola 600 at Lowe's Motor Speedway in Charlotte, North Carolina. But Jarrett retained the points lead with fifths at Charlotte and a week later at Dover, Delaware. Martin was third in both races.

On June 13, Jarrett solidified his hold on the points lead with his second victory of the season in the Kmart 400 at Michigan Speedway. Jarrett dominated the event, averaging a record 173.997 mph in his Taurus as the 400-miler was run totally under the green flag. Jarrett led from the fifty-third lap on and won by fifteen car lengths. "That's probably the best race I've ever driven," said Jarrett. "I had an almost perfect race car with no cautions to interrupt it. But sitting as a fan, I'd hate to see a race like that." Burton, who ran third, said, "Today was a blowout."

Jarrett retained his lead with a third at Pocono, Pennsylvania, on June 20, and a sixth at Sears Point. Martin, meanwhile, moved up to third with a fifth at Pocono and a second to Jeff Gordon at Sears Point.

When the tour returned to Daytona for the prime time Pepsi 400 over Independence Day weekend, Jarrett won for the third time to widen his points lead. "Things may blow up in our face, who knows?" said Jarrett. "But we've got a lot of confidence right now. I don't think we'll be getting conservative. We want to get as big a lead as we can and hopefully the end of the season will come real soon." Burton ran third at Daytona, then won the Jiffy Lube 300 at Loudon, New Hampshire, a week later, where Jarrett ran fourth.

Jarrett's climb to the top of the standings climaxed with his second victory in the Brickyard 400 at Indianapolis Motor Speedway on August 7. The Brickyard 400 was Jarrett's fourth win of the season and his fourth in eleven races. It was also the third in four races by a Taurus and No. 11 of the season. When Jarrett departed Indianapolis, he headed into the final fourteen races of the 1999 season with a 274-point lead, the biggest lead after twenty races in the NASCAR Winston Cup Series standings since Dale Earnhardt's 279-point lead in 1993 earned him the championship.

Excluding a non-points nineteenth-place finish in The Winston at Charlotte, North Carolina, Jarrett finished outside the top five only once in twelve races, from the April 25 DieHard 500 at Talladega, Alabama, to the Brickyard 400. Jarrett's run included four wins, two runner-up finishes, a third, a fourth, and three fifths. His worst points finish was a sixth on the road course at Sears Point Raceway in Sonoma.

But the triumph at Indianapolis was more than a race win. "Vindication," said Jarrett, who in 1998 was far ahead when his Robert Yates–owned Taurus ran out of gas.

"I got a feeling," said crew chief Todd Parrott. "We've got a lot of confidence in what we're doing."

Dale Jarrett had a number of triumphs to celebrate at the Indianapolis Motor Speedway on August 7, 1999. Not only did he drive his Robert Yates–owned Taurus to victory in the Brickyard 400, Jarrett widened his lead in the NASCAR Winston Cup points race to 274 points— virtually a two-race margin.

More than the technical profile of a car, the Taurus story is also about the people who make up the fifteen NASCAR Winston Cup Series teams of the Ford Racing family.

Twenty Tauruses compete regularly in the 1999 season. Five of those—Johnny Benson, Jeff Burton, Kevin LePage, Chad Little, and Mark Martin—run for Jack Roush's team. Roush-prepared Fords dominated Trans-Am road racing before Roush switched to the NASCAR Winston Cup Series in 1988 with Martin driving for the one-car program. Martin and Roush have been paired since, but the team steadily expanded—to two cars in 1992, three in 1996, four in 1997, and five in 1998.

Robert Yates fields a two-car team for drivers Dale Jarrett and Kenny Irwin. Former engine builder Yates joined the NASCAR Winston Cup Series as an owner in 1989 with Davey Allison as his driver. The pair enjoyed immediate success, winning fifteen races in their four-plus seasons. Jarrett joined the team in 1995 and has climbed steadily toward the top of the points standings.

Roger Penske co-owns a car (Jeremy Mayfield) with Michael Kranefuss and is a majority owner of a second car (Rusty Wallace) through Penske Racing South, the team that originally developed the Taurus in 1997 while also fielding Thunderbirds for Wallace and Mayfield.

The single-car teams include three owner-drivers: Bill Elliott, Ricky Rudd, and Brett Bodine. The longest association with Ford is the Wood Brothers team, who won their first race for Ford in 1960 at Bowman-Gray Stadium with Glen Wood driving.

The late Harry Melling began his association with the NASCAR Winston Cup Series in 1982 with Bill Elliott as his first driver. Together, they won thirty-four races and one championship in ten seasons.

Ricky Rudd has raced Fords since fielding his own team in 1994. In 1998, he scored a modern record with wins in sixteen-straight seasons by driving his Taurus to victory in the NAPA 500 at Martinsville, Virginia.

Ford Taruses representing three different teams battle during the 1999 Daytona 500. Leading the pack is Dale Jarrett (88) in one of two Tauruses fielded by Robert Yates. Just behind Jarrett is Rusty Wallace (2) in the Penske Racing South entry and to the inside is Jimmy Spencer (23) in the Travis Carter—owned Taurus.

Ford Racing
Highlighting NASCAR Winston Cup Teams

"I compare being part of this team to what it must be like to play on a championship baseball or football team. There's a lot of talent that runs through the Ford Taurus cars, the drivers, the engineers, and engine builders right through to anyone associated with Jack Roush."
—JOHNNY BENSON

Johnny Benson

Team–Roush Racing • Crew Chief–Paul Tryson

Benson, the 1996 NASCAR Winston Cup Rookie of the Year, is in his second season with Roush Racing. (Besides Benson, the five-car team includes Jeff Burton, Mark Martin, Kevin Lepage, and Chad Little. Last year, the Roush organization accounted for nine wins, 130 top-three finishes, and $11,158,808 in prize money.)

Benson, thirty-six, has steadily climbed his way up the ladder. A year after winning his first hometown championship in 1989, the native of Grand Rapids, Michigan, became the American Speed Association (ASA) Rookie of the Year. In 1993, he won the ASA title and a year later was Rookie of the Year in the NASCAR Busch Series, Grand National Division. He won the Grand National title in 1995 to gain an opportunity to drive a NASCAR Winston Cup Series car.

Although he finished twentieth in the final 1998 NASCAR Winston Cup Series standings, Benson ranked tenth after the Texas 500 following three top-five finishes in a six-race stretch. He was fourth in the Taurus sweep at Las Vegas; fifth at Bristol, Tennessee; and fifth at Texas Motor Speedway.

Brett Bodine

Team–Bodine Racing • Crew Chief–Gere Kennon

"When Ford first announced the Taurus was going to be the body style, I thought it was an ingenious idea. NASCAR had always gone for the traditional two-door sedan. Today's world is getting away from a need for a midsized two-door. Ford decided to go with the product of the future. It was a tremendous idea."—BRETT BODINE

Brett Bodine probably has a little more insight into the car and presentation end of racing than most drivers. Like his older brother Geoffrey, Brett advanced from modifieds to stock cars, finishing second in the final standings of the 1986 Busch Racing Series, Grand National Division. Today Brett is owner-driver of his Ford Taurus. Although he drove a season for Bud Moore in 1988, Bodine was reintroduced to Ford by Junior Johnson in 1995; he purchased the team from Johnson that same year. In 1998, Brett Bodine was voted one of the fifty greatest modified drivers of all time.

Brett Bodine topped $1 million in seasonal earnings in 1998.

Jeff Burton

Team–Roush Racing • Crew Chief–Frank Stoddard

Now in his fourth year as Mark Martin's teammate at Roush Racing, Burton is seen as one of the bright young stars in the NASCAR Winston Cup Series. He also races the Ford Taurus in the NASCAR Busch Series, Grand National Division and the NASCAR Winston Cup Series and has won races in both divisions each of the last three years. Jeff became interested in racing at age five while watching his older brother Ward race go-carts. In addition to his interest in cars, Jeff captained his high school basketball and soccer teams. Jeff won his first short-track championship at the age of twenty. His association with Ford began in 1994 with the Stavola Brothers team. After two years, he joined Roush in 1996, and in 1997 he picked up the first three wins of his career, and finished fourth in points.

Burton picked up two wins in 1998 and set personal records with eighteen top fives and twenty-three top tens.

Burton would have challenged Ford teammate Mark Martin for second in the NASCAR Winston Cup Series point standings last year were it not for four did-not-finishes.

Hut Stricklin
Team–Scott Barbour Racing • Crew Chief–Mike Hillman

"I'm blessed with a great opportunity, getting a chance to drive the new Ford Taurus for an energetic new owner like Scott Barbour."—HUT STRICKLIN

The veteran driver joined new car owner Scott Barbour and the SBIII Motorsports team midway through the 1999 season. A NASCAR Winston Cup Series driver since 1987, Stricklin is best known for his courageous run during the 1996 Mountain Dew Southern 500. Stricklin led 143 laps before his car began overheating, and he finished second to Jeff Gordon. Stricklin began his career in his native Alabama, where his heroes included Bobby and Donnie Allison. Stricklin won the Alabama State Limited Sportsman Championships two straight years (1978–79) and the NASCAR Goody's Dash Series title in 1986. He raced three seasons for Bobby Allison (1990–92) and finished a career-high sixteenth in the final NASCAR Winston Cup Series standings in 1991. Later, he spent full seasons driving for Junior Johnson, Travis Carter, Kenny Bernstein, and the Stavola Brothers.

Bill Elliott

Team–Bill Elliott Racing • Crew Chief–Wayne Orme

Bill Elliott was born into a Ford family. "Fords were all that my father drove and that's what we raced," Elliott once said. He ranks third on the all-time list of Ford winners and leads the active Ford drivers with forty NASCAR Winston Cup Series victories. Elliott raced Fords on Georgia short-tracks with brothers Dan and Ernie before joining the NASCAR Winston Cup Series in 1976. Bill won a single-season record eleven superspeedway races in 1985—a year in which he claimed the Winston Million for winning three of NASCAR's "crown jewel" races (Daytona 500, Winston 500 at Talladega, and Southern 500 at Darlington). He won the NASCAR Winston Cup Series championship in 1988 and was the runner-up in 1985, 1987, and 1992. In addition to success on the track, Elliott has been voted NASCAR's Most Popular Driver for an unprecedented thirteen straight years and he was voted the American Driver of the Year, in 1985 and 1988.

"I have never driven anything but a Ford. I've had many great moments in racing, and Ford has been with me in every one of them."—BILL ELLIOTT

Irwin opened the 1999 season on a high note by driving his Taurus to a third in the Daytona 500.

Kenny Irwin

Team–Robert Yates Racing • Crew Chief–Doug Richert

Car owner Robert Yates has an eye for driving talent. Since launching his NASCAR Winston Cup Series team a decade ago, the list of drivers in Yates Fords includes Davey Allison, Ernie Irvan, and Dale Jarrett. The lineup produced thirty-eight wins in ten years. But Yates surprised the experts before the 1998 season when he tabbed Irwin to become Jarrett's teammate. Although Irwin scored two wins and was the NASCAR Craftsman Truck Series Rookie of the Year in 1997 (finishing 10th on points), his background was in open-wheel cars on the United States Auto Club (USAC) trail. In 1996, he won the USAC Midget title and was second in the Silver Crown series. He was Rookie of the Year in all three USAC divisions before turning to NASCAR. In his NASCAR Winston Cup Series debut at Richmond, Virginia, in 1997, Irwin qualified second and finished eighth making him the only driver since 1972 to start on the front row and finish among the top ten in his first race. In 1998, Irwin was the NASCAR Winston Cup Series Rookie of the Year (his fifth rookie of the year award) and became the first rookie to win more than $1 million in his first season.

"When the call came, it was like answering the dream of a lifetime. Driving a Ford for Robert Yates is racing at its highest level."
—KENNY IRWIN

Dale Jarrett

Team–Robert Yates Racing • Crew Chief–Todd Parrott

Jarrett has been associated with some of Ford's top names—Cale Yarborough, the Wood Brothers, and since 1995, Robert Yates. Originally signed by Yates as Ernie Irvan's teammate, Jarrett quickly became one of the top drivers in the NASCAR Winston Cup Series, one of a dozen drivers with fifteen or more NASCAR Winston Cup Series victories in a Ford and two-time winner of the Daytona 500. He won seven races and finished a career-best second for Yates in 1997, and finished third in points for the second time in three seasons in 1998. In 1996, Jarrett won both the Daytona 500 and the Coca-Cola 600. The North Carolina native started racing at Hickory Motor Speedway where his father, two-time NASCAR Winston Cup champion, Ned was track promoter. Jarrett is a scratch golfer whose first dream was to play on the PGA tour.

Father Ned Jarrett ranks second with forty-three career wins in a Ford product, and he won the 1965 championship in a Ford Fairlane.

"My love of Fords goes back to when my dad was racing them. My dad and then David Pearson. Fords and Mercurys were the thing."—DALE JARRETT

Kevin Lepage

Team–Roush Racing • Crew Chief–Skip Eyler

After moving from the Buz McCall team to Roush Racing in the middle of the 1998 season, Lepage finished second in the NASCAR Winston Cup Series Rookie of the Year competition to Kenny Irwin, another Taurus driver. The son of a drag racer, Lepage named Ford legend David Pearson as the most influential person to him early in his career. And his favorite classic car is a 1938 Ford Coupe. Lepage started racing in the NASCAR Busch Series, Grand National Division in 1994. He considers winning the 1996 NASCAR Busch Series race at Homestead, Florida—before a live national television audience—the most memorable moment of his career thus far.

Lepage was the highest finishing rookie in eleven races in 1998, with a sixth in the second race at Charlotte, North Carolina, being his top finish.

"My second race in a Taurus was at Bristol, Tennessee, in 1998. We ran in the top fifteen all day and moved forward to tenth at the finish. It was a great feeling."

—KEVIN LEPAGE

Chad Little

Team–Roush Racing • Crew Chief–Jeff Hammond

The lone driver on the NASCAR Winston Cup Series with a degree in law (Gonzaga University, Washington), Little is one of the top drivers to have come out of the NASCAR Winston West Series (champion, 1987; Rookie of the Year, 1986). An all-section high school football player in Spokane, Washington, Little began racing stock cars during his freshman year at Washington State.

Little made his first NASCAR Winston Cup Series start in 1986, but had only two top-ten finishes during his first eighty-seven starts. Little gained attention in 1995 by winning the Goody's 300 at Daytona International Speedway, the first of his six NASCAR Busch Series, Grand National Division wins that season. In 1998, his first season with Roush Racing, Little finished second in the Texas 500 and had six other top-ten finishes in the NASCAR Winston Cup Series. His jump from thirty-sixth to fifteenth in the point standings was the largest posted by a driver in 1998.

Little opened the 1999 season by driving his Taurus to ninth-place finishes in the Daytona 500 and the Cracker Barrel 500 at Atlanta Motor Speedway.

"I was stoked the first time I got in a Taurus. Usually, new cars take a while to find their legs. But the Taurus showed it had promise from the start. You could tell the engineers and the test people had done their homework in the Ford tradition."
—CHAD LITTLE

Mark Martin

Team-Roush Racing • Crew Chief-Jimmy Fennig

"The association between Jack Roush, Ford, and the drivers is more one of family than a business partnership. When you think Roush, you think Ford."
—**MARK MARTIN**

When Jack Roush redirected his Ford-based racing operations toward the NASCAR Winston Cup Series in 1988, he selected Mark Martin as his first driver. The pair have been a team ever since. Martin's first NASCAR Winston Cup victory in the second race at Rockingham, North Carolina, in 1989 was also the first for Roush. Martin ranks fourth on the all-time list of Ford winners and is second to Bill Elliott among active drivers. Martin led all Taurus drivers with seven wins in the model's first season of NASCAR Winston Cup Series racing. He posted twenty-two top-five finishes and placed second in the final point standings for the third time in his career. Martin is also the all-time leader in wins on the NASCAR Busch Series, Grand National Division. When away from his Ford Taurus, Martin is an avid bodybuilder.

Mark Martin was the first driver to win a Winston Cup points race in the new Ford Taurus.

Pole firsts are Mast's forte. In addition to winning the first Brickyard 400 pole, Mast was the first driver to put a Taurus on the pole in 1998's second race at Rockingham, North Carolina.

Rick Mast

Team–Cale Yarborough Motorsports • Crew Chief–Mark Tutor

Rick Mast will forever be known for winning the pole for the inaugural 1994 Brickyard 400 NASCAR Winston Cup Series race at the Indianapolis Motor Speedway. At age sixteen, Mast traded one of his family's cows for a car so he could go racing. He won a track championship near his Lexington, Virginia, home at the age of seventeen. Mast moved up to the NASCAR Busch Series, Grand National Division in 1984 and won a total of nine races before advancing to the NASCAR Winston Cup Series in 1988. His first pole came at Atlanta in 1992, which was also Richard Petty's last race. Mast's most memorable moment was the 1989 Daytona 500. He finished sixth in an unsponsored car despite a late fuel stop. "I think I had enough gas left to go all the way and win it," he said.

> "Before the 1998 season, we built our speedway Taurus in-house. And we went to Daytona and had the fastest Taurus in the test sessions. I was very proud of that."
> —RICK MAST

Mayfield was the most consistent Taurus driver at the start of the model's first season. He led the NASCAR Winston Cup Series in points four times in the first sixteen weeks and was first or second in the standings for thirteen straight weeks.

Jeremy Mayfield

Team–Penske–Kranefuss • Crew Chief–Peter Sospenzo

A native of Owensboro, Kentucky, Mayfield began racing go-carts at age thirteen in 1982. He worked as a fabricator in a stock car shop in the early 1990s in exchange for time behind the wheel in test sessions. Mayfield was the Automobile Racing Club of America Rookie of the Year in 1993 and caught the eye of several NASCAR Winston Cup teams when the two associations ran together. Mayfield's association with Ford began with the Cale Yarborough team in 1995. Mayfield and crew chief Paul Andrews joined the then two-year-old Michael Kranefuss team in 1997, the same year Roger Penske joined the operation. Mayfield's first career victory came in the first race in 1998 at Pocono, Pennsylvania. Rusty Wallace's teammate finished a career-high seventh in the final NASCAR Winston Cup Series standings in the 1998 season.

"You always remember that car that gave you your first pole and the one that gave you your first win. Well, a Ford Thunderbird gave me my first pole, and a Ford Taurus gave me my first win."—JEREMY MAYFIELD

Ted Musgrave

Team–Butch Mock Motorsports Crew Chief–Jon Wolfe

Musgrave is a collector of rare Fords. His private museum in Daytona Beach, Florida, includes a 1956 Thunderbird, two 1959 Thunderbirds, a 1958 Custom, a 1958 Custom 300, a 1958 Ranchero, a 1958 Sedan Delivery, a 1958 Fairlane 500 Skyliner two-door with retractable roof, a 1957 retractable, and a 1958 Edsel. His wish list is topped by a 1959 retractable. "Whenever I have a couple of hours to spare, I like to go out in my barn and work on my old Fords," said Musgrave, whose hobby, if you haven't guessed yet, is restoring old cars. Musgrave has raced Fords in the NASCAR Winston Cup Series since his debut in 1990. He was the runner-up to the NASCAR Winston Cup Rookie of the Year award in 1991. He was part of the Jack Roush team from 1994 through the first part of the 1998 season. He finished seventh in the final NASCAR Winston Cup points standings in 1995.

Musgrave has five career poles, including the last ever at North Wilkesboro Speedway.

"The Thunderbird was a good race car, but it had been around so long it was like a dinosaur. What we needed was a giant step forward. The Taurus came along at the right time and gave us what we needed when we needed it."—TED MUSGRAVE

Although Nadeau didn't break into the top ten in his thirty starts last season, he had just three finishes of thirty-sixth or worse, a showing of consistency that bodes well for the future.

Jerry Nadeau

Team–Melling Racing • Crew Chief–Newt Moore

Nadeau finished third in the NASCAR Winston Cup Series Rookie of the Year standings in 1998 while driving for the Bill Elliott–Dan Marino and Melling teams. A graduate of the Skip Barber Racing School at Sears Point, California, Nadeau got his start road racing open-wheel cars. Nadeau is a ten-time champion in go-carts and was the Formula Ford Rookie of the Year in 1991. All of that might explain how he claimed the outside pole for the first time at Sears Point in 1998 and how his best finish was a fifteenth on the NASCAR Winston Cup's other road course at Watkins Glen.

"It was the first time I had ever been to Dover [Delaware]. We qualified eighth and the Taurus was perfect. We were running eighth and on the lead lap when we got tangled with lapped traffic. But the car was awesome."—JERRY NADEAU

Robert Pressley

Team–Jasper Motorsports • Crew Chief–Charlie Pressley

"When I first saw the Taurus roll out, I knew Ford had done its homework. When we first tested at Daytona, I knew it was going to be fast once the bugs were worked out."
—ROBERT PRESSLEY

The runner-up to Ricky Craven in the 1995 NASCAR Winston Cup Series Rookie of the Year race, Pressley started his career at the New Asheville and Greenville-Pickens Speedways near his North Carolina home. Pressley drove a soft drink delivery truck to support his early racing ventures. His first big break came in 1988 at the age of twenty-nine when Cleveland Cavaliers center Brad Daugherty (who also had North Carolina roots) selected Pressley to drive for the NASCAR Busch Series, Grand National Division team he purchased. Pressley won his first race the next season and advanced to the NASCAR Winston Cup Series in 1994. Pressley is in his second year with car owner Doug Bawel.

Pressley finished a career-best third in the Texas 500 at Texas Motor Speedway in 1998.

Ricky Rudd

Team-Rudd Performance Motorsports
Crew Chief-Mike McSwain

Rudd has put together one of the most impressive streaks in racing. Through the end of the 1998 season, Rudd had won at least one race in sixteen straight seasons—a modern-era NASCAR Winston Cup Series record. From 1984 to 1987, Rudd spent four seasons with Bud Moore's fabled team, winning six races and never finishing lower than seventh in the standings. Since 1994, Rudd has doubled as owner-driver, one of the most demanding combinations in sports. He finished fifth in the final 1994 standings, his first season as an owner-driver, and was ninth in 1995 and sixth in 1996. In 1997, Rudd expertly saved fuel and won the Brickyard 400 at the Indianapolis Motor Speedway. Aside from his racing, Rudd's an avid car collector; the 1932 Ford Deuce Coupe is his favorite classic car.

Rudd had to endure terrible conditions at Martinsville, Virginia, last year to keep his sixteen-year winning streak alive. Rudd won, despite the failure of his driver cooling system, on a day when the temperature soared to ninety-five and the humidity was running at 90 percent. After taking the checkered flag, an exhausted Rudd had to be helped from his car.

"I have always admired the Ford tradition, which I was a part of when I drove for Bud Moore. When I formed my own team, it had to be a Ford."
—RICKY RUDD

The twenty-four-year-old Sadler opened the 1999 season as the twenty-seventh driver to run the NASCAR Winston Cup Series under the Wood Brothers banner. In operation since 1953, the Wood Brothers have won ninety-six races. Their list of winning drivers includes David Pearson (forty-three wins), Cale Yarborough (thirteen), Neil Bonnett (nine), and Marvin Panch (eight). The Wood Brothers signed Sadler, a keen competitor for the 1999 Rookie of the Year Award. Sadler made his NASCAR Busch Series, Grand National Division debut in 1995 at the age of twenty after winning a NASCAR Winston Racing Series track championship at South Boston Speedway. He finished eighth in the 1998 NASCAR Busch Series, Grand National Division final standings.

Sadler cracked the top ten for the first time in his NASCAR Winston Cup Series career with a tenth-place finish in the 1999 Texas 500 at Texas Motor Speedway.

Elliott Sadler

Team–Wood Brothers Racing • Crew Chief–Mike Beam

"It's quite an honor to be in this car. The Wood Brothers are one of the great names in racing history. When I looked at their record, I was awestruck. They were winning races almost twenty years before I was born."—ELLIOTT SADLER

Jimmy Spencer

Team–Travis Carter Enterprises • Crew Chief–Donnie Wingo

Dubbed "Mr. Excitement" while winning back-to-back NASCAR touring titles in 1986 and 1987, Spencer joined Ford's NASCAR Winston Cup Series family in 1992 with Bobby Allison, where he had three top-five finishes in the final four races. Spencer spent the 1993 season with Allison, where he finished twelfth in the final standings before moving to Junior Johnson's team. The popular and outspoken Spencer won two races with Johnson and moved again before the 1995 season to Travis Carter's team. Spencer's potential can be seen in two top finishes (including a second in the DieHard 500) last year at Talladega—NASCAR's biggest, fastest oval. Spencer has scored three recent wins in non-points races: the 1996 Winston Open (Charlotte), the 1998 Bud Shootout Qualifier (Daytona), and the 1998 No Bull 25 (Charlotte).

In 1996, Spencer's Ford Thunderbird covered more miles than any other car in the NASCAR Winston Cup Series.

"I remember the Ford we had with Junior Johnson at Talladega in 1994 for the DieHard 500. I was in line with twenty laps to go and Junior came on the radio and said 'I believe it's time to go.' I got to the lead and my Ford beat Bill Elliott's Ford."—JIMMY SPENCER

RUSTY WALLACE
DRIVER OF THE YEAR
First Quarter 1998

"I remember when we switched to Ford. . . . I think we blew a lot of minds when we won at Rockingham in only our second race with Ford."
—RUSTY WALLACE

The Penske team was the primary development team assigned the task of preparing the Taurus for the 1998 season. "It was a thrill and an honor to be part of the development process," said Wallace. "We proved right away that all the work paid off when Jeremy was third and I was fifth in the Daytona 500." The fifth was Rusty's highest finish ever in a restrictor plate race.

At Phoenix International Raceway Wallace scored the 15th and final win of the Taurus's first season. That was Wallace's 17th victory for Ford, and it helped him finish fourth in the final NASCAR Winston Cup standings. Wallace is considered one of NASCAR's premier road racers. He won the NASCAR Winston Cup Series championship in 1989 and has twice finished second.

Wallace established a career high by winning ten races in 1994, his first season in a Ford Thunderbird. He also finished second in points that season.

Rusty Wallace
Team-Penske Racing South • Crew Chief-Robin Pemberton

After finishing twenty-first in his Ford debut at the 1999 Daytona 500, Waltrip finished twelfth in the Goody's 500 at Martinsville, Virginia.

"*Once I got involved with Ford, it didn't take long for me to be impressed with the cars, the people, and the programs. For decades, Ford has set a standard.*"—DARRELL WALTRIP

Darrell Waltrip

Team—Carter Haas Racing • Crew Chief—Philipe Lopez

Although he has spent much of his career in the rival camp, Waltrip has always had a healthy respect for Ford. "I remember walking into the Holman-Moody factory—and that's what it was—and seeing all those engines on crates waiting to be shipped," said Darrell. "Just to see all that was something. The great teams today are only duplicating what Ford was doing more than a quarter-century ago. Ford had it then, and everyone learned from what they did." Darrell entered the 1999 season with eighty-four NASCAR Winston Cup Series wins, tying him at third on the all-time list with Bobby Allison. Waltrip's three NASCAR Winston Cup Series titles came in 1981, 1982, and 1985. He was the first three-time winner of the American Driver of the Year Award (1979, 1981, and 1982). Darrell's other career accomplishments include winning a modern-era eight races from the pole in 1981 and winning the 1989 Daytona 500.

"The only way to succeed in racing is to look ahead rather than behind."

That thought by team owner Jack Roush reflects Ford's decision to introduce a remodeled Taurus for the 2000 NASCAR Winston Cup Series.

Although the Taurus enjoyed unprecedented racing success in its first two years on the track, Ford requested modifications to reflect the visual design changes in the production model Taurus being introduced in fall of 1999. The result is the "Taurus 2K."

The car will have a new look. The headlamps and front hood have been redesigned. So have the front and rear fascias, the rear window, and the trunk. The result is a striking car.

"It's always been important to Ford that the car NASCAR fans see on the racetrack looks like the one they can see on the showroom floor," said Bob Rewey, Ford group vice president for marketing, sales, and service.

Even more significant to Ford's race teams, though, are the subtle refinements made to the racing Taurus through a cooperative effort by all Ford teams and extensive wind tunnel testing. While the original Taurus was developed by Penske Racing South, the Taurus 2K was a joint effort between Ford Racing Technology and Ford's three leading NASCAR teams—Penske Racing South, Robert Yates Racing, and Roush Racing—plus input from all Ford teams.

The Taurus 2K was introduced to the public on August 4, 1999, during events leading up to the Brickyard 400 at the Indianapolis Motor Speedway—slightly more than two years after the first racing Taurus was unveiled. The Taurus 2K was track tested during fall 1999 and makes its racing debut at the Daytona 500 opener of the 2000 season.

"The Taurus 2K is the flagship car that will take Ford into its second century of racing," said Dan Davis, director of Ford Racing Technology. "We know changing over again to a new model is a challenge, but we're confident the changes made to the Taurus will keep us at the top of the championship standings."

Winston Cup points leader Dale Jarrett stands at the head of the pack as Ford drivers study the new Taurus 2K at the car's formal unveiling August 4, 1999, at Indianapolis, Indiana.

Taurus 2K
Preview of the Future of Ford